When You Lie Down & When You Rise Up

Daily Readings in B'Midbar - Numbers

Rabbi Jonathan Allen

Foreword by Rev Tim Butlin

When You Lie Down & When You Rise Up
Daily Readings in B'Midbar - Numbers
ISBN 1-901917-12-6
Copyright © 2011 Jonathan Peter Allen

Cover Design by Naomi Allen

Typeset in Times New Roman, Viner Hand, Aquaduct, Briner Pro

All rights reserved. No part of this publication maybe reproduced, stored in a retrieval system or transmitted, in any form, or by any means, electronic, mechanical, photocopying, recording or otherwise, without the prior permission of the publishers.

Where Scriptures are unattributed, they are the author's own translation. Otherwise they are attributed and taken from:

CJB	Complete Jewish Bible, Copyright © 1998 by David H. Stern. Published by Jewish New Testament Publications, Inc., Clarksville, Maryland, U.S.A. www.messianicjewish.net/jntp Used and adapted with permission.
ESV	The Holy Bible, English Standard Version, Copyright © 2001 by Crossway Books, a division of Good News Publishers. www.gnpcb.org. Used by permission. All rights reserved.
GWT	GOD'S WORD Translation. Copyright © 1995 God's Word to the Nations. Used by permission. www.godsword.org All rights reserved.
JPS	Tanakh - The Holy Scriptures, Copyright © 1985 by The Jewish Publication Society www.jewishpub.org All rights reserved.
Message	The Message by Eugene H. Peterson, Copyright © 1993-96, 2001-02. Used by permission of Navpress Publishing Group www.navpress.com All rights reserved.
NASB	New American Standard Bible, Copyright ©1960, 1962, 1963, 1968, 1971, 1972, 1973, 1975, 1977 by The Lockman Foundation www.Lockman.org Used by permission.
NIV	Holy Bible, New International Version, Copyright © 1973,1978,1984 by International Bible Society. Used by permission of Zondervan www.zondervanbibles.com All rights reserved.
NRSV	New Revised Standard Version Copyright © 1989,1995 by The Division of Christian Education of the National Council of the Churches of Christ in the United States of America. Used by permission. All rights reserved.
NCV	New Century Version Copyright © 1987, 1988, 1991 by Word Publishing, a division of Thomas Nelson, Inc. Used by permission. All rights reserved.

Published by Elisheva Publishing Ltd.
www.elishevapublishing.co.uk

Contents

	Foreword	i
	Introduction	iii
	Technicalities	v
בְּמִדְבַּר	B'Midbar - In the desert	1
נָשֹׂא	Naso - Take	23
בְּהַעֲלֹתְךָ	B'ha'alotkha - When you set up	45
שְׁלַח־לְךָ	Sh'lakh L'cha - Send for yourself	69
קֹרַח	Korakh - Korah	93
חֻקַּת	Hukkat - Statute	117
בָּלָק	Balak - Balak	139
פִּינְחָס	Pinkhas - Pinchas	155

מַטּוֹת / מַסְעֵי Mattot - Tribes / Masa'ei - Stages   177

Feast Readings

שָׁבֻעֹת Shavuot - Weeks   207

Biographies   215

Bibliography   217

Glossary   221

Foreword

It used to be that a particular young woman, Catherine Middleton, from southern England was considered 'unremarkable' and coming from a 'normal' family - that was until April this year. Since her marriage that same young woman's identity has changed radically and she is now in the British Royal Family, a duchess and wife to the second in line to the British crown. It appears that identity is everything - who we are and who we are perceived to be. Now she is pursued by a posse of photographers and her choice of a dress or hairstyle can change purchases on the high street overnight.

Our identity - who we are - in the Body of Christ, whether from a Gentile origin or an historically Jewish background, used to be of minor concern in the church at large. But since the latter part of the last millennium and the work of the Holy Spirit in the sudden rise of Messianic Judaism - Jewish believers in Jesus as Messiah preserving their Jewish identity - there has also begun a wholesale re-examination of the early church's formation and theological understanding of many New Testament writings, particularly Paul's. It appears that the largely Reformation-based approach of much Christian teaching has been called into question by this 'New Perspective', as it has become known, and in the new writings a fuller and broader Jewish understanding of the church has come to the fore.

At the time of writing, this year is the 400th anniversary of King James I's first English translation of the Bible as an Authorised Version for use in Anglican churches and the church I serve embarked on the project of reading the whole Bible in a year. Apart from the considerable advantage of reading through so much of the Word of God day after day, the most significant observable benefit to date has been the impact of reading the narrative of the people of God from the 'front of the book'. Many of us Gentile-believers give a nod to the notion that Jesus came in fulfilment to prophetic revelation, but we live as though the most important parts of our daily readings are found in the parts translated from Greek texts towards the back. The writers of those New Testament texts, and the Lord they served, were all Hebrew speakers, however, with Hebrew foundations and Hebrew thought patterns, brought up in a non-Greek culture and with a very different outlook to our own.

Jonathan Allen has done us all a great service: he has re-set our balance in favour of the approach of Jesus Himself where our understanding is built firmly upon what went before. Jesus taught from the Law and the Prophets and the 'New Perspective' keeps reminding us that the early church is an extension of a nation's calling over a thousand years before witnessed throughout the Hebrew Scriptures. More than ever we in the church are being challenged to review our identity as part of a whole body in which the foundations and culture are being re-set back to our Jewish roots.

What is distinctive about this volume, and the series of which it is a part, is that instead of arguing a case for the 'New Perspective' the writer is simply calling us into a new devotion. Here we are invited to read the *Torah* portion for the week and enter into an unfolding of insights from those who have studied and read these passages for centuries. We will find treasures from the Hebrew language, nuggets from Jewish tradition, wisdom from the Sages and, of course, the new life of the Spirit in the New Testament. This is not an 'either or' but a 'both and' devotion by which we are all enriched and are able to grow up into the single Jew-Gentile identity purposed for us in Christ. When Paul speaks of the One New Man of the people of God, made up of Jew and Gentile in Christ, he also speaks of this new theology that is both the teaching of the church's Apostles and the Prophets of old (Ephesians 2:20).

May God give us grace to be filled with wisdom and the Holy Spirit as we learn from the scope of this devotional study.

Timothy Butlin
St. Peter's Loudwater
24th June 2011

Introduction

The book of Numbers - the fourth book of the *Torah* - marks the transition between the Children of Israel receiving the words of the covenant at Mt. Sinai and their journey to *Eretz Yisrael* - the Land of Israel - as a people. Included here is the great census, of both the priests and Levites and the eleven other tribes, the abortive reconnaissance of the Land when ten of the spies brought back a bad report and the resultant circling in the desert for forty years before the children of those who came out of Egypt finally move to enter the Land. Also included is the incident when Moshe and Aharon lose their opportunity to lead the people into the Land.

Apart from the rituals of counting the people, by the lifting of the head and the half-shekel atonement, this book contains the details of the additional offerings to be brought on each of the festival days and sees the people come to the plains of Moab, across the River Jordan opposite Jericho. A whole generation of our people died in wilderness, including Moshe's sister Miriam and his brother Aharon, the first High Priest. Moshe's leadership has to stand the challenges of Korah, Dathan and Abiram, so that eventually God Himself intervenes to demonstrate His choice by the budding of Aharon's staff. Well known stories, yet here they can be seen in context and narrative order.

These commentaries on the weekly *Torah* portion have been written over the course of seven years: one per portion, per year. They have grown as we have grown; they have developed as our knowledge and understanding of the Hebrew texts, the classic and modern commentators has also developed. Like us, they are themselves a work-in-progress. They step in turn through the seven readings or *aliyot* into which the weekly portion is divided, to offer seven commentaries in each portion. You can read one at a time for each day of the week, or dip into them on an *ad hoc* basis.

These commentaries on the weekly *Torah* portion have been written over the course of seven years: one per portion, per year. They have grown as we have grown; they have developed as our knowledge and understanding of the Hebrew texts, the classic and modern commentators has also developed. Like us, they are themselves a work-in-progress. They step in turn through the seven readings or *aliyot* into which the weekly portion is divided, to offer seven commentaries in each portion. You can read one at a time for each day of the week, or dip into them on an *ad hoc* basis.

This work is, in a sense, "old hat" in that they have been published week by week on our website: *http://www.messianictrust.org.uk* and, indeed, new commentaries continue to be published each week. Please do visit the website or sign up for the weekly e-mail to join in the ongoing conversation and have your say on the thoughts presented.

We have resisted the temptation to rewrite or enlarge the earlier commentaries, believing that their value lies in what - we trust - God has been saying, rather than in the cleverness (or otherwise) of the words or the number of citations. We have nevertheless taken the opportunity to remove some spelling mistakes and typographical issues, hopefully without inserting a fresh collection during the collation and editing phase.

It is true to say that the body of Messiah outside the Messianic Jewish world has largely ignored and rejected the work of the Jewish rabbis in discussing and processing - often at great length - the words of *Torah*, God's foundational revelation to the patriarchs and the people of Israel. This has been a significant loss to the body, as many early insights into the multiple layers of meaning and nuance within the text have essentially been denied to the believing community. One of the aims of these commentaries has been to share some of the insights, commonly held among Jewish people from Second Temple times - the times of Yeshua's (Jesus') own earthly ministry - and successive generations, with the wider body of Messiah. In particular, it is our desire and - we believe - calling, to encourage our own people to re-discover the riches of the rabbinic writings and hear the ancient voices and conversations afresh in the light of our faith in Yeshua, the Jewish Messiah.

Technicalities

We usually follow the Ashkenazic division of the *parasha* into the seven readings in which the text is read during the Torah service on *Shabbat*.

As this is a work based upon the Hebrew Bible, we have followed a number of conventions of the Jewish world that may need some explanation:

a. names: we use Hebrew names for Yeshua (Jesus), Rav Sha'ul (the Apostle Paul), the patriarchs, Moshe and Aharon, the books of the *Torah* and the individual *parasha* names; this is of no doctrinal significance, but is part of our culture as Messianic Jews

Avraham	Abraham	B'resheet	Genesis
Yitz'khak	Isaac	Shemot	Exodus
Ya'akov	Jacob	Vayikra	Leviticus
Moshe	Moshe	B'Midbar	Numbers
Aharon	Aharon	D'varim	Deuteronomy

b. the chapter and verse numbering of the traditional Hebrew text: this is occasionally different from the conventional English numbering and most often only varies by one or two verses; we usually follow the numbering of the Bible version from which we are quoting; references have the English numbering in brackets if different from the Hebrew

There is one commentary for each of the seven *aliyot*; seven commentaries in each portion. These can be read one at a time for each day of the week, or dipped into on an *ad hoc* basis. Each commentary contains a short Hebrew text, its transliteration into an English character set and an English translation, followed by a commentary based upon the text, some verses or passages for further study and some application suggestions.

Leap years - the Jewish calendar has seven leap years in each nineteen year cycle, when we add an extra month to the year - often a challenge to the *parasha* sequence. In non-leap years, some of the portions are traditionally read together; in leap years, they are read separatel The reader will find that while the double portions have full coverage, the single portions do not have a full complement of seven commentaries each.

Citations from the ancient Jewish writings - the Mishnah, the Talmuds and the Midrash Rabbah are accompanied by their appropriate references.

The prefix "*m.*" means Mishnah, "*y.*" the Jerusalem Talmud, "*b.*" the Babylonian Talmud. Each part of Midrash Rabbah is given its Hebrew name, for example B'Midbar Rabbah. Talmud references give the page (or folio) number in normal type, while the side *a* or *b* in italic.

References to the classic commentators show their names in the Aquaduct font; there are brief biographical details listed for each named source in the Biography section at the end of the book. These are intended to provide a frame or context from which the commentator speaks. Author and book names also share the Aquaduct font and can be found in the Bibliography section, at the end of the book.

Terms and expressions in an italic typeface are explained in the Glossary section at the end of the book. This provides definitions of some of the other documents, languages and factual information that are referenced in the commentaries, or explain some of the terms that may be unfamiliar to modern readers or those from a less Jewish-friendly background.

Quotations from the Scriptures themselves are shown in Brinar Pro font so that they are distinct from the commentary text.

One particular Jewish convention is used with such frequency that although it has glossary entries, we felt that we should explain it here as well. It is Jewish custom not to use or pronounce the tetragrammaton covenant name of God in an inappropriate or irreverent way in order to fulfill the commandment not to take God's name in vain. Jewish custom is therefore to use one of two allusions to allow the name of God to be used and referred to in a "safe" way. Obviously, the tetragrammaton appears many times in the Hebrew biblical text. When formally read or used in a worship context, the word is pronounced *Adonai*; on other occasions it is pronounced *HaShem*, which literally means "The Name". You will find these words used in many places in the commentaries.

Every book that includes transliteration of Hebrew words into an English alphabet has its own particular style. The purpose of the transliteration is to provide a pronunciation that also reflects the different letters where possible. We denote the Hebrew letter *chaf* by 'ch', *khet* by 'kh' and *kof* by 'k'. A *chaf* with a *dagesh* (a dot in the middle of the letter) is also shown as 'k'. We represent both *sin* and *samech* by 's' and *tzadi* by 'tz'. Dipthongs are usually shown by adding an 'i' or 'y' to the ordinary vowel letter. We generally follow modern Israeli pronunciation, so *vav* has a 'v' sound and *tav* and *tet* are both always 't'. In particular we do not follow the Ashkenazic custom of pronouncing a *tav* without a dagesh as 's'.

We do not take account in this book of *Rosh Chodesh* or the "special" *shabbaton* during the year, such as *Shabbat Shekalim* or *Shabbat Shuva*, when some of the ordinary readings may be replaced by an otherwise out-of-sequence reading. Readings for the festivals will be found at the end of the normal weekly readings, before the reference sections.

בְּמִדְבַּר

B'Midbar - In the desert

B'Midbar / Numbers 1:1 - 4:20

רִאשׁוֹן	Aliyah One	B'Midbar/Numbers 1:1 - 19
שֵׁנִי	Aliyah Two	B'Midbar/Numbers 1:20 - 54
שְׁלִישִׁי	Aliyah Three	B'Midbar/Numbers 2:1 - 34
רְבִיעִי	Aliyah Four	B'Midbar/Numbers 3:1 - 13
חֲמִשִׁי	Aliyah Five	B'Midbar/Numbers 3:14 - 39
שִׁשִּׁי	Aliyah Six	B'Midbar/Numbers 3:40 - 51
שְׁבִיעִי	Aliyah Seven	B'Midbar/Numbers 4:1 - 20

B'Midbar - Numbers

בְּמִדְבַּר א'

B'Midbar - In the desert - 1

B'Midbar / Numbers 1:1 - 19

B'Midbar/Numbers 1:1 And Adonai spoke to Moshe in the Sinai Desert, in the Tent of Meeting

וַיְדַבֵּר יהוה אֶל־מֹשֶׁה בְּמִדְבַּר סִינַי בְּאֹהֶל
b'ohel Siynay b'midbar Moshe el Adonai vay'dabeyr

מוֹעֵד
mo'eyd

As we move into the fourth book of the *Torah*, we find Moshe talking with *Adonai* in the Tent of Meeting. You will recall that at the start of the third book, Vayikra, *Adonai* calls to Moshe from the Tent of Meeting - an open call which presumably others could have heard - and gives him instructions that the people are to obey regarding the different types of sacrifices. Here, as the text goes on to tell us, Moshe is given instructions that he is to obey: to take a count or census of the people. Tradition holds that the Tabernacle was erected on the first day of Aviv/Nissan, and this is now the first of Iyar. Just as it is tradition that the *mezuzot* are to be affixed to the doorpost within thirty days of a Jewish family taking up residence in a house, as it is then considered a permanent dwelling, so *Adonai* waited thirty days after taking up residence in the Tabernacle before counting the people so that everyone would know that He was there to stay: a permanent dwelling.

Now that things have settled down in the camp, the passage also tells us something about the relationship between Moshe and *Adonai*. No longer does Moshe go up a mountain or hear from God from the middle of a burning bush, but they meet in the privacy and seclusion of the Tent of Meeting. In other words, Moshe starts having regular quiet times! The text tells us that not everything is designed to happen in public - there are some things that are supposed to happen in private; one-on-one, just an individual and the Lord. Many of the great pivotal moments of faith described in the pages of the Scriptures - Avraham, Elijah, Jeremiah and others - were profoundly personal moments, just God and the person concerned: one-on-one.

So it is no surprise to find Yeshua picking up the same theme. Teaching the disciples, He says, contrasting them with the very public acts of piety of some of the Jewish leaders, "But you, when you pray, go into your room, close the door, and pray to your Father in secret. Your Father, who sees what is done in secret, will reward you" (Matthew 6:6, CJB). Times of corporate prayer, when the body comes together to seek God's face, can be incredibly powerful; one will lead in song, another will bring a scripture, yet another a word of prophecy, and all pray together - and heaven is moved; mighty things are accomplished in the heavenlies when believers gather to pray together. But, astonishing as it may seem from a human point of view, just as much happens when each one of us prays, or spends time with God. It is almost as if God puts the whole of heaven and the rest of the world on hold in order to spend precious personal moments with us. It is when we are on our own with God that He confronts, challenges and comforts us in our relationship with Him; it is then that He heals the pieces of broken days and rejoices to share our triumphs and successes.

Further Study: 1 Kings 19:9-14; Luke 6:12-19

Application: How are you doing on personal time with God? When we get busy, our quiet times with Him often get squeezed. Why not make the time today to spend in quietness with God? Get a fresh cup of tea or coffee and sit down and talk things over with Him.

בְּמִדְבַּר ב'

B'Midbar - In the desert - 2

B'Midbar / Numbers 1:20 - 54

B'Midbar/Numbers 1:20 These were the sons of Re'uven, the first-born of Israel

וַיִּהְיוּ בְנֵי־רְאוּבֵן בְּכֹר יִשְׂרָאֵל

Yis'rael b'chor R'uveyn b'ney vayih'yu

    Reuben was Ya'akov's oldest son, his first son with Leah, his first wife and the eldest daughter of Lavan. Reuben was the senior among the twelve sons of Ya'akov, the one to inherit the double portion and to lead the family in the following generation. But Reuben blotted his copybook badly: just after Rachel, Leah's sister and Ya'akov's favourite wife, died, "while Isra'el was living in that land ... Re'uven went and slept with Bilhah his father's concubine, and Isra'el heard about it" (B'resheet 35:22, CJB). Earlier, although his father didn't get to hear much about it at the time, Reuben messed up saving Yosef from the unwelcome attention of his brothers - although he managed to stop him being killed, he wasn't explicit enough to stop him being sold as a slave to Egypt. Not exactly a shining example of how a first-born should conduct himself - as acknowledged by Ya'akov when he spoke to all his sons just before he died: "Re'uven, you are my first-born, my strength, the firstfruits of my manhood. Though superior in vigour and power you are as unstable as water, so your superiority will end, because you climbed into your father's bed and defiled it" (B'resheet 49:3-4, CJB). Although even then Reuben kept the title, at a practical level, Judah - the fourth son - became the head of the family.

    Nevertheless, the *Torah* continues to describe Reuben as the first-born and to list his descendants first whenever the tribes are counted. This shows that there is a certain in-alienable something about the concept of בְּכֹר, first-born. Esav was rejected because he despised the privilege, responsibility and blessing of the first-born, selling it to his brother Ya'akov (B'resheet 25:27-34); the first-born belongs to the Lord and must be redeemed (Shemot 34:20); the first-born always inherits, even if born of a less-preferred wife (D'varim 21:15-17); Israel has a unique place among the nations as the first-born (Jeremiah 31:8(9)). Messiah was prophesied to occupy the place of first-born (Psalm 89:28(27)).

Luke takes particular care to show that Yeshua was Mary's first-born: "While they were there, the time came for her to give birth; and she gave birth to her first child, a son" (Luke 2:6-7, CJB). Luke then goes on to record that Joseph and Mary "took Him up to Yerushalayim to present Him to Adonai (as it is written in the Torah of Adonai, 'Every first-born male is to be consecrated to Adonai')" (v22-23, CJB) and the ceremony of *Pidyon ha'Ben* - 'redeeming the son' (v 25-35). There is no mistake that Yeshua was a physical first-born. Rav Sha'ul says, "He is the invisible God, the first-born of all creation ... He is the beginning, the first-born from the dead; so that He Himself might come to have first place in everything" (Colossians 1:15, 18, NASB).

Further Study: Psalm 89:20-30(19-29); Romans 8:26-29

Application: Among all the other facts that we learn as we study God's word, it is easy to lose sight of the fact that Yeshua is the first-born, not only of God, but among us. He is not our equal, although He is our friend. He is the head of God's household, although He is our brother. Do you need an attitude adjustment in this area?

בְּמִדְבָּר ג'

B'Midbar - In the desert - 3

B'Midbar / Numbers 2:1 - 34

B'Midbar/Numbers 2:2 each man by his banner, in the signs of the house of their fathers

אִישׁ עַל־דִּגְלוֹ בְאֹתֹת לְבֵית אֲבֹתָם
avotam   l'veyt   v'otot   dig'lo   al   iysh

    Rashi tells us that "every division shall have for itself a sign, a coloured sheet of cloth, hanging in it ... each of a different colour ... like the colour of his stone on the breastplate of *Cohen Gadol* ... so that each individual will recognise his division." Any individual could therefore find his way about the camp - a huge area, as it enclosed several million adults, children and animals, at least the size of a good-sized town - by seeing the signs hung up to demarcate the different tribal, clan and familial groupings. At times of trouble, each tribe would gather around their banner to meet or stand ready to act together as a group.

    In our first armed clash in the Exodus from Egypt, at Rephidim, our people fought a battle against Amalek. Aharon and Hur had to hold Moshe's hands up in the air as a banner over the people until sunset and the people had defeated Amalek; so Moshe "built an altar, and named it 'The Lord is My Banner'" (Shemot 17:15, NASB) because the Lord was a sign, a focus, a rallying point and inspiration for the people. Writing in the Psalms, David said, "You have given a banner to those who fear You, that it may be displayed because of Your truth" (Psalm 60:4, NASB). Like the Royal Standard of England - an enormous flag - flown over Windsor Castle or Buckingham Palace when the Queen is in residence, God has given His people a banner, to be seen by all, to show that His presence is with, dwells among, them.

    Every time the *Shemoneh Esrei* is recited, at each prayer service in the day, we say, "Sound the great *shofar* to herald our freedom; raise high the banner to gather our exiles. Gather our dispersed from the ends of the earth" (Sim Shalom) reflecting two texts from the prophet Isaiah: "On that day a great shofar will sound. Those lost in the land of Ashur will come, also those scattered throughout the land of Egypt; and they will worship Adonai on the holy mountain in Yerushalayim" (Isaiah 27:13, CJB) and "And He shall set up an ensign for the nations, and shall assemble the outcasts of Israel, and gather together the dispersed of Judah from the four corners of the earth" (Isaiah 11:12, KJV). The latter, of course, is part of the great prophecy of the Messiah starting at the beginning of the chapter with the Rod that comes from the stem of Jesse, the Branch.

We see that re-gathering taking place before our eyes - as it has been for the last sixty years - God slowly gathering His people, our people, back to the Land of Israel. At the same time, more and more Jewish people are coming to know and recognise Yeshua as the Messiah of Israel, so that there are now more followers of Yeshua in the Land than at any time in history since the first century CE. At still the same time, huge numbers from the nations are discovering that Yeshua is their Messiah too, especially in the non-Europeanised world: Africa, Asia, South America. God is surely doing a great work in these days, establishing His Son as a banner for our people and for all the nations.

Further Study: Ezekiel 37:15-28; Matthew 24:27-31

Application: Sometimes we get so caught up in the detail of our daily lives that we miss the huge moves that are taking place on the world stage. Today would be a good day to step back from the coal-face and take a good look at just how much God is doing in our day!

בְּמִדְבַּ֜ר

B'Midbar - In the desert - 4

B'Midbar / Numbers 3:1 - 13

B'Midbar/Numbers 3:1 And these are the generations of Aharon and Moshe in the day Adonai spoke to Moshe on Mt. Sinai

וְאֵ֛לֶּה תּוֹלְדֹ֥ת אַהֲרֹ֖ן וּמֹשֶׁ֑ה בְּי֗וֹם דִּבֶּ֧ר יהוה
Adonai diber b'yom ooMoshe Aharon toldot v'eyleh

אֶת־מֹשֶׁ֖ה בְּהַ֥ר סִינָֽי׃
Siynay b'har Moshe et

    Strangely, this verse introduces only a list of the four sons of Aharon and does not mention any sons of Moshe. Why should this be? Rashi comments: "It mentions none but the sons of Aharon, yet they are called 'offspring of Moshe' because he taught them *Torah*. It teaches us that whoever teaches his friend's son *Torah*, Scripture views him as of he had fathered him." This is based upon the Talmud which records: "Rav Samuel ben Nahmani said in Rav Jonathan's name: He who teaches the son of his neigbour the *Torah*, Scripture ascribes it to him as if he had begotten him, as it says, 'Now, these are the generations of Aharon and Moshe'; whilst further on it is written, 'These are the names of the sons of Aharon', thus teaching that Aharon begot and Moshe taught them, hence they are called by his name" (b. Sanhedrin 19b). Since by the time that Rav Samuel said this there were schools in every town, organised by Joshua ben Gamala, we can tell that this referred to a serious teaching or discipling role rather than just school or rote learning of the texts at an elementary level.

    We find the same idea at work in the relationship between Rav Sha'ul and Timothy. Although Sha'ul and Timothy were not physically related - the book of Acts tells us that Timothy "was the son of a Jewish woman who had come to trust, and a Greek father" (Acts 16:1, CJB) and was started in the faith by his grandmother Lois and mother Eunice (2 Timothy 1:5) - yet Rav Sha'ul writes, "To Timothy, my dear son" (2 Timothy 1:2, CJB) and "Timothy, my true child in the faith" (1 Timothy 1:2, NASB). What is this link that has formed between them? Sha'ul had taken Timothy under his wing and become a spiritual mentor and father to him. He attended to Timothy's circumcision (Acts 16:3) and taught him *Torah*, both The *Torah* and the *Torah* of Yeshua. This is why, writing to Timothy some years later, Sha'ul could say, "the things you heard from me, which were supported by many witnesses, these things commit to faithful people, such as will be competent to teach others also" (2 Timothy 2:2, CJB). Throughout the Pastoral Epistles we find Sha'ul urging both Timothy and Titus to develop their teaching ministries, to come alongside others and develop those deep father-son teaching and mentoring relationships.

The Master, of course, did the same. Yeshua spent three years with His disciples, teaching them the *Torah* - the gospels record a number of occasions, such as Matthew 5-7, where Yeshua was clearly teaching the meaning of *Torah* to not only His closest disciples but also the crowd who had gathered to hear His teaching. He sometimes refers to the disciples in that way: "Children, how hard it is to enter the kingdom" (Mark 10:24, NASB), or "Children, you do not have any fish, do you" (John 21:5, NASB), demonstrating that aspect of His relationship with the twelve.

We should be endeavouring to build the kingdom by developing relationships with people, coming alongside them and teaching them the words of *Torah*. The ancient rabbis said, "make many disciples" (Pirkei Avot 1:1) and Yeshua Himself gave that charge to the disciples in the Great Commission (cf. Matthew 28:18-20).

Further Study: Galatians 3:6-9; 1 Corinthians 4:14-17

Application: How many spiritual children do you have? Are you working on encouraging those people that you know to become disciples of Yeshua and to learn His *Torah*? Why not pray during this week that you will have an opportunity to come alongside someone to do just that.

בְּמִדְבַּר ה'

B'Midbar - In the desert - 5

B'Midbar / Numbers 3:14 - 39

B'Midbar/Numbers 3:15 You shall count all the males from one month old and upwards

כָּל־זָכָר מִבֶּן־חֹדֶשׁ וָמַעְלָה תִּפְקְדֵם:

tif'k'deym vama'lah khodesh miben zachar kol

After the main census of the people that *HaShem* had instructed Moshe and Aharon to take, they are now told to count the tribe of Levi who had been excluded from the larger survey of their brothers. Whereas the other tribes were counted "from twenty years old and upwards, whoever is able to go out to war in Israel" (B'Midbar 1:3, NASB), the tribe of Levi was numbered from infancy and included all males regardless of fitness. The Sages tell us that "the Levites were numbered on this occasion for the sole purpose of redeeming the firstborn" (B'Midbar Rabbah 3:8): as the *Torah* later says about the firstborn of the other tribes - "from a month old you shall redeem them" (B'Midbar 18:16, NASB), so the Levites are numbered from one month old. Other commentators suggest that perhaps due to the incidence of neo-natal mortality, a child was not considered viable until it was at least a month old.

Rashi borrows the description שֹׁמְרֵי מִשְׁמֶרֶת הַקֹּדֶשׁ - guardians of the watching of the sanctuary - from verses 28 and 32 below, to comment that "once he leaves the category of newborn, he is counted to be called 'one who safeguards the guarding of the holy.'" Even though they do not formally enter the service of the Tabernacle until the age of thirty, because of their role in the redemption of the firstborn and their potential to serve when older, they are considered as part of the body of Levites that are responsible for preserving the holiness of the sanctuary. Rabbi Samson Raphael Hirsch, seeking another reason why the Levites below the official minimum age of service were counted, points to the Talmud where it recounts that although not allowed to make up the official number of Levites standing on the platform to sing, the younger boys and men were encouraged to join in and support the singing during the worship in the

Temple (b. Arachin 13b).

Hirsch goes further than this specific role for under-30 year old Levites: "This counting of the Levites from earliest infancy ... can be taken to prove that the calling of the Levites goes far beyond the service of the Sanctuary ... a calling from which perhaps they are fit at an earlier age, but which must demand the whole of the bringing up and education of the youths from earliest childhood onwards." Hirsch points out that the Levites not only had charge of the physical material of the Tabernacle: the furniture, the curtains, the vessels; they "were to be the defenders and protectors, teachers and advocates of the *Torah* itself and its observance." This follows Moshe's blessing of the tribe of Levi: "For they have observed Your word and kept Your covenant. They shall teach Your ordinances to Jacob, and Your law to Israel" (D'varim 33:9-10, NASB). For the Levites to teach successfully, this had to be a whole lifetime and lifestyle issue; they were the paramount living example, strategically sited throughout the Land, in the midst of the people to show by their lives and teach by their words, the way that *Torah* was to be lived. Every Levite child, then, was to learn *Torah* from the earliest moment and the behaviour and the conduct of the Levite families - fathers, mothers, children - were all a part of the larger mission to teach the Children of Israel as a whole. As God said: "Be careful ... that you diligently observe and do according to all that the Levitical priests shall teach you; as I have commanded them, so you shall be careful to do" (D'varim 24:8, NASB).

Rav Sha'ul emphasises this when he writes to Timothy concerning the qualifications for leadership in the body of Messiah. Only too well aware of living in a goldfish bowl, he says that an overseer "must be one who manages his own household well, keeping his children under control with all dignity" (1 Timothy 3:4, NASB), while deacons must be "husbands of only one wife, and good managers of their children and their own households" (v. 12, NASB). Writing to Titus he is even more explicit about elders: "above reproach, the husband of one wife, having children who believe" (Titus 1:6, NASB). It is a specific requirement for leaders that their children must be able to support their father, both in faith and practice, and that it is a critical proof of his calling that he has demonstrated his abilities in his own family. Of course, children must be allowed to be children and to have fun according to their age - this is essential to a balanced life and upbringing. Families in ministry are to demonstrate the proverb: "Train up a child in the way he should go, even when he is old he will not depart from it" (Proverbs 22:6, NASB).

What then are we set apart for? Who is looking at us and counting? The simple - and perhaps shocking - answer is: everyone! In these days when there is heightened interest in spirituality, when people are seeking some meaning and purpose in life, we are under the spotlight all the time.

Whether we like it or not, whether we feel ready or not, we are being observed constantly by those around us who want to know whether we are for real of just faking it like so many others in the world. Even as new believers, we are counted pretty much from day one, and the way we live our lives, raise our families, run our finances, even down to doing our gardens, are under constant scrutiny from those who are desperate to find the truth, hoping - even though they appear critical - that we may be able to help them. Whether physical Levites or called by Yeshua to be "the salt of the earth" (Matthew 5:13), we are both called and counted!

Further Study: 2 Chronicles 17:7-9; Matthew 5:13-16

Application: Do you count for other people or yourself? Think today of how you can count for others and help them to see the Kingdom of God in you. Ask God what you do that counts and what else He wants you to do so that your "count" can increase.

בְּמִדְבָּר ו'

B'Midbar - In the desert - 6

B'Midbar / Numbers 3:40 - 51

B'Midbar/Numbers 3:40 Count every first-born male among the sons of Israel from one month old ...

פְּקֹד כָּל־בְּכֹר זָכָר לִבְנֵי יִשְׂרָאֵל מִבֶּן־חֹדֶשׁ
khodesh mi'ben Yisra'el livney zachar b'chor kol p'kod

וָמָעְלָה
vama'lah

    The first word in the text - פְּקֹד - is a *Qal* ms imperative from the root פָּקַד, a verb that has an extensive range of connected meanings. Davidson lists nine distinct meanings for the *Qal* stem alone, including "to visit; to punish; to review, muster, number; to look after or take care of; to set over or appoint". As the immediate text is followed by the instruction to "take account of their names", this suggests that this is a more detailed or even intimate counting than the numbers alone might indicate. The resulting count of first-born males is 22,273 from a total army population of 603,550 (cf. B'Midbar 1:46), which Jacob Milgrom correctly points out is a difficult proportion as it would "presume an average Israelite family of fourteen male children." Even 22,273 is a substantial number of men to individually count and know and it would seem to predicate a fairly perfunctory and mechanical counting process if it were not for the mention of the individual names.

    The phrase בֶּן־חֹדֶשׁ - literally, 'son of a month' - is a typical instance of a class of biblical Hebrew phrases used to denote ages for both people and animals. Moshe is described as "the son of eighty years" and Aharon his brother as "the son of eighty three years" (Shemot 7:7) when they are called to appear before Pharoah to present *HaShem*'s demand that he let the people of Israel go free from Egypt. When establishing the liturgy and ritual for *Yom HaBikkurim*, the Day of early First-fruits, the priests are told, "Now on the day when you wave the sheaf, you shall offer a male lamb one year old without defect for a burnt offering to the Lord" (Vayikra 23:12, NASB); once again, the lamb is literally, "the son of his year". Suspecting a high infant mortality rate among the Israelites in the desert, after their recent release from Egypt, Rashi comments that this command excludes new-born sons who, although circumcised on their eighth day, might not survive as long as a month, so should not be counted as permanent members of society. The practice of not counting, or in many cases not naming for some months, new-born children persisted even in western societies until early in the nineteenth century. Although children often didn't survive until adulthood, it was considered unwise to form too close an emotional attachment to or waste a traditional family name on a baby until they had proved a certain level of viability.

Hirsch points out that the exercise being carried out by Moshe and Aharon at this point is unique; this is the only time that the first-born of Israel as a group are redeemed by the Levites. While *HaShem* has previously told Moshe "every first-born of man among your sons you shall redeem" (Shemot 13:13, NASB), the exact way this was to be done didn't come until several chapters after this point in the narrative: "Every first issue of the womb of all flesh, whether man or animal, which they offer to the Lord, shall be yours; nevertheless the first-born of man you shall surely redeem, and the first-born of unclean animals you shall redeem. And as to their redemption price, from a month old you shall redeem them, by your valuation, five shekels in silver, according to the shekel of the sanctuary, which is twenty gerahs" (B'Midbar 18:15-16, NASB). This ceremony is known as *Pidyon ha'Ben* and is still practised today, by taking the child to a *cohen* - a Jew who is of priestly descent - and giving him a number of coins and asking him to bless the baby. In modern times, the money is usually not retained by the *cohen* but is used to start a savings account in the child's name for when they become an adult. The Greek Scriptures record an occasion when it was observed during Second Temple times: "There was in Yerushalayim a man named Shim'on. This man was a tzaddik, he was devout, he waited eagerly for God to comfort Isra'el, and the Ruach HaKodesh was upon him. It had been revealed to him by the Ruach HaKodesh that he would not die before he had seen the Messiah of Adonai. Prompted by the Spirit, he went into the Temple courts; and when the parents brought in the child Yeshua to do for Him what the Torah required, Shim'on took Him in his arms, made a b'rakhah to God, and said, 'Now, Adonai, according to Your word, Your servant is at peace as You let him go; for I have seen with my own eyes your yeshu'ah (salvation), which you prepared in the presence of all peoples - a light that will bring revelation to the Goyim and glory to your people Isra'el.' Yeshua's father and mother were marvelling at the things Shim'on was saying about Him. Shim'on blessed them and said to the child's mother, Miryam, 'This child will cause many in Isra'el to fall and to rise, He will become a sign whom people will speak against; moreover, a sword will pierce your own heart too. All this will happen in order to reveal many people's inmost thoughts'" (Luke 2:25-35, CJB). Yeshua Himself was a first-born male!

In the verse following our text, Moshe is told, "And you shall take the Levites for Me, I am the Lord, instead of all the first-born among the sons of Israel, and the cattle of the Levites instead of all the first-born among the cattle of the sons of Israel" (v. 41). The service of the Levites is taken in place of the redemption that should - had the instructions been given in time - have been made for the first-born in all the other tribes when they were born.

The importance of the first-born in the mind of the people continued through the early days in the Land. Influenced by the remnant of the Canaanite peoples who had not been expelled from Israel, some of the people offered their children to pagan gods as child sacrifices. During the days of the kings, Josiah - a reforming king who tried to make the people turn back to *HaShem* - "defiled Topheth, which is in the valley of the son of Hinnom, that no man might make his son or his daughter pass through the fire for Molech" (2 Kings 23:10, NASB). One of the prophets asks, "Does the Lord take delight in thousands of rams, in ten thousand rivers of oil? Shall I present my first-born for my rebellious acts, the fruit of my body for the sin of my soul?" (Micah 6:7, NASB)

Rav Sha'ul explains that Yeshua is "the image of the invisible God, the first-born of all creation" (Colossians 1:15, NASB). More, Sha'ul goes on, "He is head of the Body, the Messianic Community - He is the beginning, the firstborn from the dead, so that He might hold first place in everything" (v. 18, CJB). Yeshua's first-born status is more than just being the first-born of Mary His human mother; He is also the only begotten Son of God, His first-born, who is from eternity to eternity. He is the model God uses to shape us who believe in Him, so that Yeshua should be the head of a family of brothers and sisters sharing His life: "because those whom [God] knew in advance, He also determined in advance would be conformed to the pattern of His Son, so that He might be the firstborn among many brothers" (Romans 8:29, CJB). This is also the order for the resurrection: "Messiah has been raised from the dead, the first fruits of those who are asleep ... each in his own order: Messiah the first fruits, after that those who are Messiah's at His coming" (1 Corinthians 15:20,23, NASB).

Moshe was told to count the first-born among the children of Israel, in a personal way, taking note of their names. Yeshua, who has been given the name that is above all names, is the first-born not only of Israel but of all creation and He has been raised first from the dead. Uniquely, since several people have been raised back to life after dying, but subsequently died again, Yeshua was restored to life for ever, for He is "the Resurrection and the Life" (John 11:25). Because He lives, we live and will live for ever in Him and He knows each of our names!

Further Study: John 6:39-40; Revelation 1:17-18

Application: How can you know more of the power of Yeshua's resurrection life in your life today? Know that you have been counted individually and that He knows your name; take fresh hold of the promise that you are already being changed into His image, to be like Him; be inspired that His resurrection - a certain and immutable fact - means that you will live forever in Him! Now, that's life!

בְּמִדְבַּר ז'

B'Midbar - In the desert - 7

B'Midbar / Numbers 4:1 - 20

B'Midbar/Numbers 4:3 ... from the age of thirty years and upwards until fifty years, anyone coming to the workforce ...

מִבֶּן שְׁלֹשִׁים שָׁנָה וָמַעְלָה וְעַד בֶּן־חֲמִשִּׁים
khamishiym ben v'ad vama'lah shanah sh'loshiym miben
שָׁנָה כָּל־בָּא לַצָּבָא
latzava ba kol shanah

The first thing to note in this text is that the words for the numbers thirty and fifty look like three and five in plural; this is a standard Hebrew technique: used in the singular, the numbers three to nine are exactly that, three to nine; when plural they represent the decades thirty to ninety, hence thirty and fifty. At the same time, the noun שָׁנָה is singular; this is another standard construction: obviously if there is only one of an item, it is represented by a singular noun; as expected, if there are two to ten of an item, then the noun is usually plural; if, however, there are more than ten items then the noun is usually singular.

A second point of interest is that the lower age is not the same in Septuagint translation of this verse. There the text reads ἀπὸ εἴκοσι καὶ πέντε ἐτῶν - from five and twenty years. Scholars think that this was probably done by a scribe or translator who wanted to harmonise this text - specifically given for the descendants of Kohath, one of the three non-priestly clans of the Levites - with the general rule given for all the Levites a few chapters later: "This is the rule for the Levites. From twenty-five years of age up they shall participate in the work force in the service of the Tent of Meeting; but at the age of fifty they shall retire from the work force and shall serve no more" (B'Midbar 8:24-25, JPS). The Sages comment in the *Midrash* (B'Midbar Rabbah 6:7) that this verse can be used to confirm the statement made in the Mishnah "a thirty-year-old attains full strength" (*m. Pirkei Avot* 5:25). Rashi adds that "one who is less than thirty, his strength has not become fully developed ... and one who is more than the age of fifty, his strength diminishes from then on."

Thirdly, Jacob Milgrom makes a comment about the particular choice of language used at the end of our text: בָּא לַצָּבָא implies non-military service, as opposed to יֵצֵא לַצָּבָא which has the sense "go to war" as found at the start of this *parasha*: "Take a census of all the congregation ... whoever is able to go out to war in Israel" (B'Midbar 1:2-3, NASB). Milgrom suggests that the verb בָּא - from the root בוֹא, to come or enter - bears the technical meaning of "qualify", so that the phrase could mean "all those who are qualified". This implies that the work to be done is skilled labour rather than physical labour; that the Kohathites would require more skill in carrying the holy - and lethal, if mishandled - items from the sanctuary than their colleagues in the other clans who carried the physical structures of the Tabernacle (boards, sockets, curtains and coverings) and so might account for the later age for starting service.

The Sage's comment about the age of thirty seems also to be borne out also in the case of Yosef, the favourite son of Ya'acov, who was sold by his brothers, as a rather brash youth at around the age of 17 or 18, into slavery in Egypt. After twelve years - first serving Potiphar, followed by some years in prison - he became the Prime Minister of Egypt. How old was he? "Yosef was thirty years old when he entered the service of Pharaoh king of Egypt" (B'resheet 41:46, ESV). The years of service and servitude were necessary to prepare him for the position of leadership. Through those years, God was teaching him wisdom, tact, diplomacy, strength of character, endurance and the other essential skills that he would need in such a high place of authority and ministry. At thirty, he came into his full strength of manhood and was ready to take on the job to which he had been called.

David was the youngest of eight brothers and was chosen as a youth to be King Saul's musician and armour-bearer. After defeating the Philistine champion Goliath, he became very popular among the people and was perceived as a threat to the king. He then spent perhaps as long as ten years leading a raggle-taggle band through the desert, including a period of sojourning among Israel's enemies the Philistines and one incident of feigning madness, before Saul died. "David was thirty years old when he became king" (2 Samuel 5:4, NASB). In the meantime, as we know from both the narrative and many of the psalms which David wrote during that time, David's leadership skills and abilities were refined and honed in a furnace of real affliction so that when time came, he would be ready to step up and be God's anointed king over the people of Israel and Judah.

A thousand years later, a descendant of David also spent years preparing for a crucial public ministry. Born into an artisan household, he was known as "the carpenter's son" (Matthew 13:55, CJB) and "the carpenter, the son of Mary" (Mark 6:3). The word translated "carpenter" is τέκτων, with a range of meanings from "builder" to "woodworker", so probably also included working with stone, masonry and mortars as well as in wood. Living in a small town in the Galil, he and his father Joseph would probably have been employed in one of the larger building projects of the time as Herod Antipas built his capital at Zippori/Sepphoris, around an hour's walk from Nazareth. Working on a busy construction site would have given plenty of opportunities to learn not only physical but also interpersonal and leadership/management skills as well as precision and judgement. As a child, He "became strong and filled with wisdom - God's favour was upon Him" (Luke 2:40, CJB); as He moved through His teenage years, He "grew both in wisdom and in stature, gaining favour both with other people and with God" (v. 52, CJB). Tradition tells us that His father died, leaving Him to support the family on his own, possibly teaching His brothers the building trade and to earn money for the family. A tough call by today's standards: long, hard and potentially dangerous physical work, walking to and from work, supporting a mother and a large family of siblings, constantly exercising skill and judgement to stay well and safe, running and discipling a family. God was preparing Him for a life of destiny and challenge where He would need those skills and experience.

Then, when He reached the fullness of His strength, He answered the call that God had placed upon His life. Stepping out of the village of Nazareth, He began preaching and proclaiming the Kingdom of God throughout the Galil. Luke's gospel tells us that "Yeshua was about thirty years old when He began His public ministry" (Luke 3:23, CJB). From there, He chose a small group of close disciples, developed a level of financial support and amassed crowds of eager followers as He travelled the roads of Judea and the Galil to visit towns, cities and individual homes. A number of years of teaching and ministry culminated in the master pivot point of history - His victory over death - through His crucifixion and resurrection in Jerusalem. The hours of on-the-job discipleship, the miracles of healing and supernatural provision, the fervour of the last prayers in the Garden of Gethsemane, the silent submission to false arrest and execution, were all made possible by the years of preparation "and being made perfect, He became the source of eternal salvation to all who obey Him" (Hebrews 5:9, ESV).

God still prepares people for His service today. Rav Sha'ul spent some years in Arabia after becoming a believer before he visited the apostles in Jerusalem; Timothy travelled with Sha'ul to "learn the ropes" before being sent off on his own missions. We can and should expect God to continue to work in the same way. As Sha'ul wrote, "For whom He fore-knew, He also predestined to become conformed to the image of His Son, that He might be the first-born among many brethren; and whom He predestined, these He also called; and whom He called, these He also justified; and whom He justified, these

He also glorified" (Romans 8:29-30, NASB), describing the process that takes place in each believer's life - being transformed into the image of Yeshua.

Further Study: 2 Corinthians 9:8; Ephesians 3:20-21

Application: Where is God working in your life? What is He doing today to prepare you for tomorrow? Are you answering that call, working with Him, no matter what that may entail, knowing that His plan and purpose are bigger than anything you can image, "both to will and to work for His good pleasure" (Philippians 2:13, NASB)? If not, why not?

Naso - Take

B'Midbar / Numbers 4:21 - 7:89

רִאשׁוֹן	Aliyah One	B'Midbar/Numbers 4:21 - 37
שֵׁנִי	Aliyah Two	B'Midbar/Numbers 4:38 - 49
שְׁלִישִׁי	Aliyah Three	B'Midbar/Numbers 5:1 - 10
רְבִיעִי	Aliyah Four	B'Midbar/Numbers 5:11 - 6:27
חֲמִשִׁי	Aliyah Five	B'Midbar/Numbers 7:1 - 41
שִׁשִּׁי	Aliyah Six	B'Midbar/Numbers 7:42 - 71
שְׁבִיעִי	Aliyah Seven	B'Midbar/Numbers 7:72 - 89

Naso - Take - 1

B'Midbar / Numbers 4:21 - 37

B'Midbar/Numbers 4:22 Take a census of the sons of Gershon, them as well ...

נָשֹׂא אֶת־רֹאשׁ בְּנֵי גֵרְשׁוֹן גַּם־הֵם
heym gam Geyrshon b'ney rosh et naso

Curiously, the command 'take a census' literally means 'lift the head', so that the phrase could be translated: lift the head of the sons of Gershom, also them. The same word combination is also used for several other meanings, for example, to cheer someone up. When people are sad, their heads are cast down and by relieving their distress, by cheering them up, you lift their heads and enable them to be happy again. Similarly, apart from the sadness of slavery, someone who is a slave or even a servant is expected to carry themselves in a respectful way, not holding their head up as a free man would but with their head down to indicate their submission - when they are given their freedom, then their heads are lifted as they once more join the ranks of those who are not beholden to others. We see another two meanings in the word-play of Yosef interpreting dreams in prison in Egypt: in B'resheet 40:13, the cup-bearer is told that Pharaoh will lift up his head and restore him to his place of honour, whereas in verse 19 the baker is told that Pharaoh will lift his head right off him - having him executed.

David the king said, "But You, Adonai, are a shield for me; You are my glory, You lift my head high" (Psalm 3:4, CJB), or as the older versions have it, "You are my glory and the lifter of my head" (KJV). He wrote this at the time when he had been forced to flee from Jerusalem by his own son, Absalom. Fleeing for his life, David recognised that is was God who gave him not only his joy and his freedom, but also his dignity and position as king over Israel. In acknowledging that, he is set free in his spirit and his face is lifted to and by God. In another of David's psalms, he says, "Lift up you heads, O gates, and be lifted up, O ancient doors, that the King of Glory may come in" (Psalm 24:7, NASB); that even the gates and doors of the Temple, of the world, may form a guard of honour and stand to attention as the King comes through.

Yeshua uses the image of freedom when He speaks of His return in glory, "When these things start to happen, stand up and hold your heads high; because you are about to be liberated" (Luke 21:28, CJB). The signs in the sky, the behaviour of the nations, the shaking of the powers in the heavens all tell us that Yeshua is about to return, and we are to lift our heads because He is coming to set us free!

When our faces are downcast, we cannot see what is going on around us, others cannot see our faces and we project an image of slavery, sadness and depression. God wants to lift our heads so that we can cheer up in Him, being secure in His love for us, so that we may know His truth and be set free, so that we may conduct ourselves as children of the King.

Further Study: Psalm 121:1-8; John 12:32

Application: Have you become weary with the pressure of every day life and allowed your head to become downcast? Today is a good day to know the exhilaration of God's love and promises for you - let Him lift your head and see your face.

נָשֹׂא ב׳

Naso - Take - 2

B'Midbar / Numbers 4:38 - 49

B'Midbar/Numbers 4:38 And the numbered men of the sons of Gershon by their families, and by their fathers' households ...

וּפְקוּדֵי בְּנֵי־גֵרְשׁוֹן לְמִשְׁפְּחוֹתָם וּלְבֵית אֲבֹתָם
avotam ool'veyt l'mish'p'khotam Geyr'shon b'ney oof'kudey

The first word of the text is a *Qal* participle translated by various Bibles as "the numbered men" (NASB), "the counted ones" or even "the census" (CJB). The root verb, פָּקַד, has a rich range of meanings, from which we can learn some interesting perspectives.

The first meaning offered by the dictionary is "visit, go or come to see". This could show that this counting was not simply a mechanical head-count, done at a distance, on an anonymous basis; this idea is re-inforced by the text telling us that the counting was done by families and ancestral households. Those counted were known individuals, each with a name and an individual personality. "I am calling you by your name; you are Mine" (Isaiah 43:1, CJB).

The second meaning is "examine, prove" and the third is closely related: "review, muster, number". These meanings suggest that each individual could have been tested or assessed - that his ability to do the work of service in the *Mishkan* was known, possibly that his attitude to doing the work could have been considered. Just as "God loves a cheerful giver" (2 Corinthians 9:7, NASB), so He wants people to serve Him willingly and in a good spirit.

The next two meanings are closely matched. The fourth meaning is "look after, take care of". Is there a sense in which God had already taken care of these men? He had brought them out of Egypt, preserved them through the desert, enabled them to stand for Him during the episode of the Golden Calf and placed them in families. On the other hand, the fifth meaning is "set over, appoint" - in the same way as those men had been looked after, they were appointed to look after those in the other tribes. The *Torah* tells us that the Levites were to be spread throughout the people of

Israel without any formal land inheritance of their own, so that they could be available to teach all the other tribes the *Torah* and pass on the traditions of *Adonai*. "We can encourage others in whatever trials they may be undergoing with the encouragement we ourselves have received from God" (2 Corinthians 1:4, CJB).

The last meaning the dictionary provides is "deposit, lay up" and this speaks of the investment that *HaShem* was making in these men. Not only were they counted and chosen, but they were to be trained and equipped for service, given skills in carrying out the tasks assigned to them. God wasn't going to throw them in at the deep end and expect them to sink or swim - He was looking at them as the deposit, laid up to bring a return on His investment. They have been set apart for Him. Yeshua said to His disciples, "You did not choose Me, but I chose you and appointed you that you should go and bear fruit and that your fruit should abide" (John 15:16, ESV).

Further Study: D'varim 7:6-9; 1 Corinthians 1:26-30

Application: Have you been visited by God? If so, then know that you have not only been visited but examined and reviewed, that you are being taken care of so that you can take care of others, and that God has invested His very self in you so that you may invest in others and bring a return of His investment in you.

Naso - Take - 3

B'Midbar / Numbers 5:1 - 10

B'Midbar/Numbers 5:2 and they shall send out from the camp anyone with tzara'at, having a discharge or unclean from [touching] a body

וִישַׁלְּחוּ מִן־הַמַּחֲנֶה כָּל־צָרוּעַ וְכָל־זָב וְכֹל
v'chol zav v'chol tzaru'a kol hama'chaneh min viyshal'khu

טָמֵא לָנָפֶשׁ:
lanafesh tamey

    The Ramban, Nachmonides, comments: "After Moshe had erected the Tabernacle, God commanded that the impure should be sent away from the camp in order that the camp should be holy and fit for the divine presence to rest therein, this being a commandment which was applicable immediately and in all subsequent generations." Rashi tells that, although out of sequence with the biblical narrative, this command was given to Moshe on the day the Tabernacle was erected - rather than a month later as the narrative would suggest - on the grounds that surely *HaShem* would not have allowed the impure to enter the sanctuary for even a day (Mizrachi, Sifsei Chachamim).

    From the moment that the Tabernacle was set up and the presence of God came down to dwell among our people, it was necessary for those who were impure to leave the camp - away from God's immediate presence - because the pure and the impure cannot mix; God is holy and cannot tolerate sin. Just as Rudolph Guiliani turned around the city of New York when he was mayor by his tough and uncompromising zero-tolerance policy against all forms of crime, from guns and shootings down to graffiti and even chewing-gum on the pavements; just as some teenagers have a zero tolerance policy towards spots and acne, the only way to combat impurity is to counter and reject it at every level. So the prophet says, "Depart, depart, go out from there; touch no unclean thing; go out from the midst of her; purify yourselves, you who bear the vessels of the Lord" (Isaiah 52:11, ESV). He is speaking to a people still to be in captivity, for when they are about to be released, ready to return from Babylon to rebuild the temple in Jerusalem; God was calling those who would carry the vessels and utensils from the temple sanctuary to purify themselves before they took up their loads for the journey.

This passage is quoted by Rav Sha'ul in 2 Corinthians 6 where he is speaking about the basic incompatibility between Messiah and the devil, between light and darkness, between believers and non-believers. Sha'ul is teaching the believers that they need to make a change in their lives, now that Messiah has taken up residence in their hearts. He writes, "For we also once were foolish ourselves, disobedient, deceived, enslaved to various lusts and pleasures ... But when the kindness of God our Saviour and His love for mankind appeared, He saved us" (Titus 3:3-5, NASB). He is firmer still with the Colossians: "Therefore consider the members of your earthly body as dead to immorality, impurity, passion, evil desire and greed ... put them all aside: anger, wrath, malice ..." (Colossians 3:5,8, NASB). When Messiah has come, we cannot continue to live in the ways of the past, but like the Israelites in the desert, must send away all impurity out of the camp.

Further Study: Colossians 3:5-10; Philippians 4:12-13

Application: Do you still struggle with things of the past - old habits and behaviour that are not pleasing to God? Now is the time to make a clean break and rid yourself of these things which drag you down. Take a firm stand, renounce them today and put them behind you, for you were called to better things.

Naso - Take - 4

B'Midbar / Numbers 5:11 - 6:27

B'Midbar/Numbers 5:12 Any man, if his wife goes astray and will commit a sin against him ...

אִישׁ אִישׁ כִּי־תִשְׂטֶה אִשְׁתּוֹ וּמָעֲלָה בוֹ מָעַל:
ma'al   vo ooma'alah ishto   tis'teh   kiy iysh iysh

 This text introduces the passage that deals with the *sotah*, a woman suspected of adultery by her husband. Our Sages (in this case, Resh Lakish) said: "A person does not commit adultery unless a spirit of folly enters into him" (*b*. Sotah 3a). The Talmud points out that the verb תִשְׂטֶה, she will go astray, is spelled the same way in the consonantal text as תִשְׁטֶה, she will act foolishly. Rashi connects this with the verse, "The one who commits adultery with a woman is lacking sense; he who would destroy himself does it" (Proverbs 6:32, NASB). By quoting this verse, Rashi shows that anyone who commits adultery, male or female, is lacking in sense.

 Hirsch, taking this a step further, quotes the verses, "Do not enter the path of the wicked ... turn away from it and pass on" (Proverbs 4:14-15, NASB) where the root שָׂטָה means not only turning aside from the way in a physical sense but also in a moral sense: turning away from a prescribed moral road. The root is used in Aramaic to mean turning away from the right mental way, towards insanity, so that Jastrow has examples from the *Midrash*, the Talmud and later rabbinic writings showing a range of meanings such as "to be demented, to be mad or insane". Hirsch combines these to conclude that every moral lapse is at the same time a mental one for, since he considers that moral truth and logical truth coincide, no man sins unless he has first lost the true conception of things. Put another way, what man or woman would commit adultery with their partner in the same bed - which would demonstrate a very altered perception of reality.

 Support for the idea that sin happens when we are not aware of or are distracted from the truth comes from the record of the very first sin: "Then the Lord God said to the woman, 'What is this you have done?' And the woman said, 'The serpent deceived me, and I ate'" (B'resheet 3:13, NASB). Rav Sha'ul confirms this when he writes, "it was not Adam who was deceived, but the woman who, on being deceived, became involved in the transgression" (1 Timothy 2:14, CJB). Eve ate the fruit of the tree that was forbidden because the Adversary, as the serpent, lied to her and made her doubt the truth of God's word. Yeshua says of the Devil "there is no truth in him ...for he is a liar, and the father of lies" (John 8:44, NASB). Each morning, near the start of the *Shacharit* prayer service, echoing the words Yeshua taught the disciples when they asked Him to teach them to pray (Matthew 6:9-13), we pray, "May it be Your will, Lord our God and God of our ancestors, to accustom us to Your *Torah* and make us attached to Your commandments. Lead us not into error, transgression, iniquity, temptation or disgrace" (Authorised Daily Prayer). We ask God to show us the truth of His word and His commandments and to keep us away from error or deception that could confuse us and so make a way for sin.

Yeshua told the disciples, "If you love Me, you will keep My commands; and I will ask the Father, and He will give you another comforting Counsellor like Me, the Spirit of Truth, to be with you forever" (John 14:15, CJB). There is a symmetry between keeping God's commandments and the presence of the *Ruach HaKodesh* - the Holy Spirit. The Spirit leads us into truth; gives us a clear view, as it were, of reality; makes us aware of our motives and sometimes the motives of others; reveals the feelings of our hearts; gives us discernment. He does this so that we can make good and accurate decisions about situations and be able to obey God's commands in any circumstance; without Him we are blind. God wants us to know the truth so that we do not go astray and sin against Him.

Further Study: 2 Corinthians 11:2-3; Proverbs 23:23; John 8:32

Application: Do you struggle with obeying God all the time? Does sin seem to come so easily some days? You need the truth to be able to see the reality of the kingdom and avoid sin. Ask God today to open your eyes and show you how things really are!

Naso - Take - 5

B'Midbar / Numbers 7:1 - 41

B'Midbar/Numbers 7:1 And it was on the day Moshe finished erecting the Tabernacle

וַיְהִי בְּיוֹם כַּלּוֹת מֹשֶׁה לְהָקִים אֶת־הַמִּשְׁכָּן
hamish'kan et l'hakiym Moshe kalot b'yom vay'hiy

Although Biblia Hebraica Stuttgartensia shows no textual variation at this point, agreeing with the Masoretic Text, it is clear that there have been variants at this point in the past. The word כַּלּוֹת, according to Davidson and Even-Shoshan, is a *hapax legomenon* in this form - a *Pi'el* infinitive construct - although it comes from the well-known root כָּלָה, to complete, finish or end. We know that a variant text was in circulation because Rashi's comment (below) is based upon a text that omits the ו to be כַּלֹּת, which in turn could be pointed and pronounced כַּלַּת, the construct form of the word כַּלָּה, a bride. The Rashba also confirms the existence of a text spelled like that of Rashi, although there is no current textual evidence today.

Rashi's comment, then, says: "כַּלֹּת is written as if כַּלַּת which implies that on the day of the erection of the Tabernacle, Israel was like a bride who enters the marriage canopy." Tanchuma adds that "the Tabernacle was like a marriage canopy, under which Israel joined God" (Tanchuma 26). Both of these comments portray the traditional view of Israel being chosen as a bride for God Himself, with the *Torah* given at Sinai being the *ketubah* - the marriage contract - and the marriage being celebrated in the Tabernacle as the *chuppa* or marriage canopy. On the day that Moshe finished erecting and preparing the Tabernacle for service, Israel is pictured as the bride about to enter the canopy to be joined to her husband in a holy covenant.

The whole verse reads: "On the day when Moshe had finished setting up the Tabernacle, and had anointed and consecrated it with all its furnishings, and had anointed and consecrated the altar with all its utensils" (NRSV), so the

Sforno comments that the altar and its vessels were set up in their proper place and order; the holiness of the moment demanded that everything should be done properly. Hirsch amplifies that idea by adding that the holiness of the whole depended on the holiness of the parts, yet the parts could not be holy apart from the whole: "the whole cannot do without even its least important part; nothing is superfluous for the whole, nothing is without meaning." To erect a canopy for the bride to meet her husband, everything had to be together, in its correct place, and perfect.

HaShem used the image of the bride and bridegroom to speak to the people of Judah during the time of the kings. Firstly, speaking of the period of time that was to come He said, "Moreover, I will take from them the voice of joy and the voice of gladness, the voice of the bridegroom and the voice of the bride, the sound of millstones and the light of lamps. And this whole land shall be a destruction and a horror, and these nations shall serve the king of Babylon seventy years" (Jeremiah 25:10-11, NASB). Yet a few chapters later, still before Jerusalem fell to the Babylonians, Jeremiah hears the Lord say, "Yet again there shall be heard in this place - of which you say, 'It is a waste, without man and without beast,' that is, in the cities of Judah and in the streets of Jerusalem that are desolate, without man and without inhabitant and without beast - the voice of joy and the voice of gladness, the voice of the bridegroom and the voice of the bride, the voice of those who say, 'Give thanks to the Lord of Hosts, for the Lord is good, for His lovingkindess is everlasting, and of those who bring a thank offering into the house of the Lord. For I will restore the fortunes of the land as they were at first" (33:10-11, NASB). The presence of the bride and bridegroom, the celebration of marriage, is a sign that the Lord is making in the Land and among our people, both then and now.

Another prophet, Amos, who also spoke during the time of the kings before the captivity in Babylon, seemed to have a longer time-scale vision. Seeing a time when God would send "a famine on the land, not a famine for bread or a thirst for water, but rather for hearing the words of the Lord" (Amos 8:11, NASB), a time that seems very descriptive of the days we live in, Amos hears the Lord say, "In that day I will raise up the fallen tabernacle of David, and wall up its breaches; I will also raise up its ruins, and rebuild it as in the days of old" (9:11, NASB). God will once again prepare a place for marriage, a tabernacle where He may celebrate with His bride. There, although ancient, God Himself will have repaired the fabric and raised the roof so that everything may be set in order and be perfect for the wedding.

So it is that we hear Rav Sha'ul speaking about Yeshua who - as a model for marriage between husbands and wives - "loved the church and gave Himself for her; that He might sanctify her, having cleansed her by the washing of water by the word, that He might present to Himself the church in all her glory, having no spot or wrinkle or any such thing; but that she should be holy and blameless" (Ephesians 5:25-27, NASB). In these days, Messiah

Yeshua is preparing His bride: "that He might redeem us from every lawless deed and purify for Himself a people for His own possession, zealous for good deeds" (Titus 2:14, NASB). Everything will be set in order, the holiness of the whole depending on all the parts who come together to make up the whole.

Further Study: Isaiah 61:10; Revelation 19:7-10

Application: Are you preparing for the wedding? Is everything set in order and its proper place in your life, your family and your congregation? God is building up the fallen tabernacle and the day is drawing near, so why not ask Him what you should do to prepare so that you will be ready for the wedding!

Naso - Take - 6

B'Midbar / Numbers 7:42 - 71

B'Midbar/Numbers 7:42 On the sixth day, the leader of the sons of Gad, Elasaf the son of D'ueyl ...

בַּיּוֹם הַשִּׁשִּׁי נָשִׂיא לִבְנֵי גָד אֱלְיָסָף
El'yasaf Gad livney nasiy hashishiy bayom
בֶּן־דְּעוּאֵל׃
D'ueyl ben

    This is the sixth of twelve identical offerings brought, once the Tabernacle has been set up and commissioned into service, by the leaders of the twelve tribes. The Levites do not bring a gift as they are already set apart as a tribe for the service of God, but both of the half-tribes of Joseph - Ephraim and Manasseh - are counted, keeping the tally to twelve. The text describing these offerings (B'Midbar 7:12-83) is highly formulaic, each of the twelve blocks starting with the day number, followed by an almost identical list of ritual items, vessels, incense and sacrificial animals, bracketed by the name of the individual tribal leader. Only very minor variations in spelling and word order - usually not seen in translation - separate the twelve lists which are obviously designed to show strong unity and commitment between the tribes and their leaders.

    Jacob Milgrom comments that the animals that were part of the offering (one young bull, one ram, one lamb, one goat, two oxen, five rams, five male goats and five year-old lambs) were not offered on the altar, but used to create a sacrificial store. Milgrom bases this comment on the animals themselves: some were peace offerings, while others were sin offerings; some were only offered on specific feast days. So, in just the same way as the basin, bowl and ladles were not offered on the altar but taken into the general service of the Tabernacle, so the animals - not given for sacrifice on that very day, but to the service of the Tabernacle - could have been used to form a stock of animals that were later available for special occasions.

    Nachmanides explains that the rabbis found (B'Midbar Rabbah

13-14) a special reason for the offering of each tribe, given the subsequent history of the tribe. "It is for this reason", he continues, "that Scripture treated them all equally, giving the details of each as if the others had not been mentioned, then together, to hint that each thought of their offering at the same time and independently." Rabbi Hirsch confirms this idea: "Each tribe represented a special kind of social activity, and its being purified and penetrated with the spirit of *Torah* and using its activities in making the demands of the *Torah* a reality, formed a completely essential specialised contribution for accomplishing the common mission of the nation."

Rav Sha'ul tells us that, "there is neither Jew nor Gentile, neither slave nor freeman, neither male nor female; for in union with the Messiah Yeshua, you are all one" (Galatians 3:28, CJB). Although we are all different people - with different callings, genders and social circumstances - yet in Messiah we are all one, we all stand on the same spiritual ground. "For by grace you have been saved through faith; and that not of yourselves, it is the gift of God; not as a result of works, that no one should boast. For we are His workmanship, created in Messiah Yeshua for good works, which God prepared beforehand, that we should walk in them" (Ephesians 2:8-10, NASB); it is by faith alone that we are in good standing with God, by receiving His gracious offer of forgiveness and life in Yeshua. The charge sheets on which we were arraigned and the basis on which our cases have been handled are all identical: a serial sinner; guilty as charged; forgiven and pardoned, bound over to keep the peace. Or as Rav Sha'ul puts it: "For all have sinned and fall short of the glory of God ... the wages of sin is death, but the free gift of God is eternal life in Messiah Yeshua our Lord" (Romans 3:23, 6:23, NASB).

Yeshua told His disciples a parable about the kingdom of God: "The kingdom of heaven is like a treasure hidden in the field, which a man found and hid; and from joy over it he goes and sells all that he has, and buys that field" (Matthew 13:44, NASB). Just like the twelve tribal leaders, to come into relationship with God costs each of us the same, no matter what resources we have: everything! What we bring is conditioned upon what we have and, to some extent, what we will be, but we bring ourselves and so no-one brings more and no-one brings less. God loves each of us enough to provide a saviour; Yeshua loved each of us enough to die for us. He doesn't value any of us any more or any less than any other.

That said, each of us has a different background, each of us has been given different skills and abilities, each of us is a different colour or shape and has been specifically called and chosen to work with a different group of people in similar but different ways. Rav Sha'ul again: "Whenever you come together, let everyone be ready with a psalm or a teaching or a revelation, or ready to use his gift of tongues or give an interpretation; but let everything be for edification" (1 Corinthians 14:26, CJB). If everyone comes to worship God all wanting to sing the same psalm, it will get boring after the first few times through. Instead, some bring a psalm, some a hymn or another spiritual song, some a verse of encouragement from the Scriptures, some a word of prophecy or even a sermon. In the blend of gifts the Spirit weaves a harmony of high and low voices - melody, bass-line and descant - and, yes, sometimes plainsong sung in unison; a mixture of voices lifted together to praise God and to declare His wonders. Whatever we bring to worship, from a grunt to a whistle, a mellow contralto to a gruff baritone, even silent sighs, we bring everything we have and God is pleased to receive the thoughts and intentions of our hearts, counting all the verbal or non-verbal contributions as the same.

The Jewish writings even record a supposed argument between the tribes as to which order they should bring their offerings, in patriarch birth order or in camp travelling order. That seems strangely reminiscent of a certain argument between the Yeshua's *talmidim* as to which one of them was the greatest or should sit at Yeshua's right and left hands - isn't it funny how the same themes crop up again in different generations! In the same way, just as the tribal princes each brought their gifts on subsequent days, so congregations don't have two or three worship leaders trying to lead worship in the same session; two or three rabbis don't try and deliver sermons at the same time. We each have to take our turn in being used by God as He sees fit. As instruments, the bassoon and the double-bass have very few concertos or solo pieces written exclusively for them and they are rarely heard distinctly in the orchestra, but their presence underpinning the sound of most classical pieces would be instantly missed if they were not playing. The player may only have a moment of distinction once in a whole concert, but must always have his eyes on the conductor so that he is ready to play, louder or softer as the maestro commands.

So we should always be in state of readiness, with our eyes fixed on Yeshua (Hebrews 12:2), to speak the word He has given us, to console or pray for the person He puts in our path, to rejoice with or rebuke a fellow believer at the Master's call. We need to keep our ears open to hear those same encouragements, challenges, remonstrance or praise being directed at us from the Lord via other members of the Body when they too play their part. "So let's not be asleep, like the rest are; on the contrary, let us stay alert and sober" (1 Thessalonians 5:6, CJB), because "those who stay alert and keep their clothes clean ... won't be walking naked and be publicly put to shame!" (Revelation 16:15, CJB).

Further Study: 1 Corinthians 12:14-26; 1 Peter 4:7

Application: Do you feel neglected or left out in the Lord's economy? Do you worry that you can make no contribution or that your time will never come? Be encouraged that everyone is essential to the whole, that without you, we are incomplete. Ask the Lord to show you today what part you are to play and then keep your eyes firmly fixed on Him and wait for His directions - it may be sooner than you think!

Naso - Take - 7

B'Midbar / Numbers 7:72 - 89

B'Midbar/Numbers 7:89 And when Moshe came to the Tent of Meeting to speak with Him, then he heard the voice speaking to him

וּבְבֹא מֹשֶׁה אֶל־אֹהֶל מוֹעֵד לְדַבֵּר אִתּוֹ וַיִּשְׁמַע
vayishma   ito   l'dabeyr mo'eyd ohel   el   Moshe oov'vo
אֶת־הַקּוֹל מִדַּבֵּר אֵלָיו
eylayv   midabeyr   hakol   et

The word מִדַּבֵּר offers some fascinating insights into the way that God speaks to or engages with mankind. This particular form - a masculine singular *hitpa'el* participle from the root דָּבַר, to speak - only occurs three times in the Hebrew Scriptures: here and twice in the book of Ezekiel. In the verse "And as He spoke to me the Spirit entered me and set me on my feet; and I heard [Him] speaking to me" (Ezekiel 2:2, NASB) the word 'Him' is not present in the Hebrew text; similarly, in "Then I heard [one] speaking to me from the house, while a man was standing beside me" (Ezekiel 43:6, NASB), the word 'one' is not present. Both are pronouns supplied by the translators as subjects for the participles, the same function as the word הַקּוֹל - the voice - plays in our text above. The *hitpa'el* stem usually conveys the idea of a reflexive or a repetitive action; for example the root שָׁעַע, meaning to close, stroke, caress, in *hitpa'el* means to delight oneself, to be dazzled or blinded.

The commentators are not happy about the idea of God speaking to Himself, for a number of reasons. First, there is the general consensus that it is improper that God should be thought of as speaking to Himself, as if this were mumbling or a sign of absent mindedness! *Targum Onkelos*, as usual, is unhappy with the anthropomorphism and, supported by Ibn Ezra, changes the verb to "that was speaking". Rashi and Sforno, on the other hand, confirm that God was speaking to Himself as a means of communicating with Moshe, so that Moshe overheard, rather than being directly spoken to -

thus avoiding the issue of God directly speaking to a human being. The Sforno comments "it is by elucidating out loud to Himself that *HaShem* imparts knowledge and goodness to others through the generosity of His influence", while Rashi adds, "It is the honour of the One who is Above to speak in this way: He communicates to Himself and Moshe would hear on his own."

Some scholars think that although the *Masoretes* had an alternative pointing available - which would have meant simply "the voice was speaking" - they refused to use it in case this might give any credence to the idea that "the voice" might be a separate divine being or identity that could speak for or as God. *Targum Jonathan* goes as far as paraphrasing the text into "Moshe heard the voice of the Spirit that was speaking to him" to avoid any allusion to John's gospel: "In the beginning was the Word ..." (John 1:1), while the Septuagint inserts the word - "of the Lord" - into the text to show whose voice was speaking. It seems clear that rabbinic Judaism wanted to clarify the meaning of this text so as to protect the unity of God and to exclude the possibility of there being another personality within the Godhead.

Hirsch, on the other hand, is more concerned about why the voice spoke to Moshe. He quickly points out, "God did not allow His Word to come to Moshe because of some special personal relationship of Moshe to God, but only as a result of the Divine bond of proximity with Israel, as a result of the Presence of God in the midst of a people keeping His *Torah*." Hirsch wants to deny that Moshe hears from God as a result of personal relationship, but rather on the basis of being simply the spokesperson of Israel; Moshe, indeed any Jew, is nothing special by himself and has contact with God only in the context of a community that maintains relationship with God on the basis of keeping the *Torah*. Again, this view may be driven by attempts to repudiate both the Christian claim of personal relationship with God in Yeshua and that God would speak to any individual rather than just to the appointed leader of a *Torah* observant community. This is a standard position for orthodox Jewry to take today.

By contrast, we know from the Scriptures that God speaks both to individuals and communities, to the saved and the unsaved, to Jew and to Gentile. His communication does not have to be based upon relationship, although it usually is. God spoke to Nebuchanezzar, the king of Babylon (Jeremiah 25:9), calling him "My servant" and to Cyrus, the Persian king (Isaiah 44:28), calling him "My shepherd". He speaks to nations: "'And I will make you [Tyre] a bare rock; you will be a place for the spreading of nets. You will be built no more, for I the Lord have spoken,' declares the Lord God" (Ezekiel 26:14, NASB) and, of course, to individuals such as Avraham, "Abram fell on his face, and God talked with him, saying, 'As for Me, behold, My covenant is with you, and you shall be the father of a multitude of nations'"

(B'resheet 17:3-4, NASB), and Ya'akov "Then God said to Jacob, 'Arise, go up to Bethel, and live there; and make an altar there to God'" (B'resheet 35:1, NASB). Yeshua spoke to the Pharisees, "Now while the Pharisees were gathered together, Yeshua asked them a question" (Matthew 22:41, NASB), to the Sadducees, "Now there came to Him some of the Sadducees (who say that there is no resurrection), and they questioned Him" (Luke 20:27-28, NASB), to the scribes, "And some of the scribes answered and said, 'Teacher, You have spoken well'" (Matthew 20:39, NASB) and to the people: "And He began to tell the people this parable" (v. 9, NASB). Yeshua also spoke to soldiers, "And when He had entered Capernaum, a centurion came to Him ... and He said to him, 'I will come and heal him'" (8:5-7, NASB) and to lepers: "And behold, a leper came to Him ... and He stretched out His hand and touched him, saying, 'I am willing; be cleansed'" (vv. 2-3, NASB); to children, "And He took them in His arms and began blessing them, laying His hands upon them" (Mark 10:16, NASB) and to His disciples, "But these things I have spoken to you, that when their hour comes, you may remember that I told you of them" (John 16:4, NASB). He even found a few words for the women in the crowd who followed Him out to be crucified, "And there were following Him a great multitude of the people, and of women who were mourning and lamenting Him. But Yeshua turning to them said, 'Daughters of Jerusalem, stop weeping for Me, but weep for yourselves and for your children'" (Luke 23:27-28, NASB).

The Scriptures are very clear that this is God speaking: "God, after He spoke long ago to the fathers in the prophets in many portions and in many ways, in these last days has spoken to us in His Son, whom He appointed heir of all things, through whom also He made the world" (Hebrews 1:1-2, NASB). Yeshua links His own words to those of God when He said, "For I did not speak on My own initiative, but the Father Himself who sent Me has given Me commandment, what to say, and what to speak. And I know that His commandment is eternal life; therefore the things I speak, I speak just as the Father has told Me" (John 12:49-50, NASB). Yeshua told us that God would continue to speak to us, through the Holy Spirit, "However, when the Spirit of Truth comes, He will guide you into all the truth; for He will not speak on His own initiative but will say only what He hears. He will also announce to you the events of the future" (John 16:13, CJB), and He continued to speak to the first believers: "I, Yeshua, have sent My angel to give you this testimony for the Messianic communities" (Revelation 22:16, CJB).

So what should we expect today? Does God still speak to His people now? Rav Sha'ul is very clear that He does: "And let two or three prophets speak ... For you can all prophesy one by one, so that all may learn and all may be exhorted" (1 Corinthians 14:29,31, NASB). Peter wrote "And so we have the prophetic word made more sure, to which you do well to pay attention" (2 Peter 1:19, NASB). We can expect God to continue to speak to us through His word - that is, the written word, the Bible - and by His Spirit, through people around us - and not just believers, God often uses those in the world to deliver surprisingly accurate messages if we will but listen. To have relationship with God mandates an ongoing conversation, as we speak to Him and He speaks to us, as we exchange views and concerns and as we know His presence in our lives. This is not a sterile and academic belief in past history, but a living relationship with God Himself!

Further Study: Job 4:12-16; Zechariah 4:4-9; John 3:31-34

Application: How do you hear from God? Is it the "still small voice" (1 Kings 19:12, KJV) when you are being quiet with Him; is it through the pages of the Bible, prophetic words or your elders or leaders? Make no mistake though, God wants to dialogue with you. Why not start the conversation today?

בְּהַעֲלֹתְךָ

B'ha'alotkha - When you set up

B'Midbar / Numbers 8:1 - 12:16

רִאשׁוֹן	Aliyah One	B'Midbar/Numbers 8:1 - 14
שֵׁנִי	Aliyah Two	B'Midbar/Numbers 8:15 - 26
שְׁלִישִׁי	Aliyah Three	B'Midbar/Numbers 9:1 - 14
רְבִיעִי	Aliyah Four	B'Midbar/Numbers 9:15 - 10:10
חֲמִשִׁי	Aliyah Five	B'Midbar/Numbers 10:11 - 34
שִׁשִּׁי	Aliyah Six	B'Midbar/Numbers 10:35 - 11:29
שְׁבִיעִי	Aliyah Seven	B'Midbar/Numbers 11:30 - 12:16

בְּהַעֲלֹתְךָ א'

B'ha'alotkha - When you set up - 1

B'Midbar / Numbers 8:1 - 14

B'Midbar/Numbers 8:2 Speak to Aharon and say to him, 'When you kindle the lamps ...'

דַּבֵּר אֶל־אַהֲרֹן וְאָמַרְתָּ אֵלָיו בְּהַעֲלֹתְךָ
b'ha'alotcha   eylayv   v'amar'ta   Aharon el   dabeyr

אֶת־הַנֵּרֹת
haneyrot et

    From the English translation, we would have expected the Hebrew verb used here to be דָּלַק, which in the *Hif'il* stem means 'to kindle or set on fire' as we find in the blessings recited when lighting the candles at *Hanukkah*: לְהַדְלִיק נֵר שֶׁל חֲנֻכָּה, *l'hadliych neyr shel Hanukkah*. Instead, we find the verb עָלָה, which in its simple form means 'to go up or ascend' and from which the modern word *'aliyah'* - going up to live in the Land of Israel - is derived. In its *Hif'il* stem, as used here, it becomes causative: Aharon is told to make or cause the lights to rise up. Rashi comments that in order to make sure that the light is burning properly, it is necessary to kindle - hold the fire to the wick - for long enough that the flame rises from the light of its own accord; the light has been caused to rise.

    God tells the prophet Ezekiel to prophesy to the scrublands of the Negev, "I will light a fire in you ... a blazing, unquenchable flame that will scorch every face ... All humanity will see that I, Adonai, lit it; it will not be put out" (Ezekiel 21:3-4, CJB). God lit a fire to raise up an unmistakable sign. He made sure the fire was large enough that it couldn't be put out - the fire was raised up to be unquenchable.

    It is common among believers to talk of God raising up leaders, missionaries, teachers or other functions within the body - a recognition that it is God who calls and equips His people to accomplish the things that He has purposed. Indeed, the process of ordaining men as pastors and elders is simply man recognising what God has already done - other leaders lay hands on those who God has already raised up to occupy these positions.

But God has not only raised up leaders - He has raised up each one of us. Each of us has been raised to spiritual life in Yeshua, and will be raised up by Yeshua on the last day (John 6:40).

The most significant act of raising that has ever been carried out is when God raised Yeshua from death. As Rav Sha'ul says, "But now Messiah has been raised from the dead, the first fruits of those who are asleep" (1 Corinthians 15:20, NASB). God caused Him to be raised from death, not only that death should be defeated and stripped of its power, but to demonstrate God's victory over sin and death through the obedience of the cross and because death could not hold Yeshua. It is when we "confess with our mouths and believe in our hearts that God raised Him from the dead" (Romans 10:9) that we are raised by God. He applies the fire of the *Ruach HaKodesh* to us until the light is raised up in us.

Further Study: 2 Corinthians 4:6-10; Matthew 5:14-16

Application: How is God's fire burning in your life? Is your relationship with God simply smouldering, a gentle flame or is it an unquenchable blaze for all to see? How can you kindle a fresh flame of enthusiasm for God?

בְּהַעֲלֹתְךָ ב'

B'ha'alotkha - When you set up - 2

B'Midbar / Numbers 8:15 - 26

B'Midbar/Numbers 8:15 And after this the Levites shall come to serve the Tent of Meeting

וְאַחֲרֵי־כֵן יָבֹאוּ הַלְוִיִּם לַעֲבֹד אֶת־אֹהֶל
ohel   et   la'avod hal'viyim   yavo'u cheyn va'akharey

מוֹעֵד
mo'eyd

    Reading this text in isolation, one would have to ask: after what? What is it that qualifies the Levites to serve the Tent of Meeting? The answer is found in the preceeding verses, and starts with being taken from among the rest of the people (v. 6), being sprinkled with the water of lustration (v. 7), shaving their whole bodies (v. 7), washing their clothes (v. 7), bringing sin offerings (v. 8), coming near before *Adonai* (v. 10), accepting Aharon's authority (v. 13), being themselves a wave offering to *Adonai* (v. 13) and finally being declared separate from the rest of Israel to be holy to the Lord (v. 14). Then, and only then, are they fit to come and do the work of service in the Tent of Meeting.

    In those eight steps we can see a foreshadowing of the process of becoming a believer. First of all there is the calling out process as *HaShem* singles us out. Hirsch groups the next three steps as a mechanical separation of self and the past. Normally, the sprinkling to remove the contamination of touching dead bodies (acquired when they killed 3,000 of the other tribes during the Golden Calf incident) is to be followed by a second sprinkling one week later, but in this case is substituted with being shaved over the whole body - quite a public denial of self, dignity and shedding one's past life. The bringing of the sin offerings can be allied to formal repentance and confession of sin - required before the sin offering could be accepted - and essential for us as believers to be able to accept God's forgiveness in Messiah Yeshua.

    At this point the Levites had to come near before *Adonai* and accept the authority of Aharon the *Cohen Gadol* and the priests in general to be told what to do and when to do it. As believers, we cannot stand at a distance having simply said "Sorry" and asked for forgiveness, we have to accept Yeshua as Lord as well as Saviour. We need to accept Yeshua as the ultimate authority in our lives and commit to obeying Him in all things. Having drawn near before *Adonai* and accepted the authority of the priesthood over them, the Levites then stood before the Lord and were themselves a wave-offering - from the people - to be the portion of the sacrifice that belonged to the priests. Believers too are to be an offering (see Romans 12:1), a spiritual sacrifice constantly being offered to God.

The last step before actually starting their service in the Sanctuary was for the Levites to hear and accept the declaration of their new state - separate from the other tribes and set apart for God. As believers, we need to walk through the process of "transforming your minds" and not being "conformed to this world" that Rav Sha'ul describes in Romans 12:2 onwards. Yeshua prayed for the disciples, "They do not belong to the world, just as I do not belong to the world. Set them apart for holiness by means of the truth" (John 17:16-17, CJB).

Further Study: John 17:6-19; 1 John 2:15-17

Application: Where do you stand against that list of steps to being fit for service in the Kingdom of God? Have you made that separation from the world and past life? Have you drawn near to God and stood before Him in Messiah Yeshua? Have you accepted Yeshua's authority in your life? Do you live a life 'in but not of' the world? Today is a day for moving forward!

בְּהַעֲלֹתְךָ 'ג

B'ha'alotkha - When you set up - 3

B'Midbar / Numbers 9:1 - 14

B'Midbar/Numbers 9:2 And the Children of Israel shall make the Pesach offering in its appointed time.

וְיַעֲשׂוּ בְנֵי־יִשְׂרָאֵל אֶת־הַפָּסַח בְּמוֹעֲדוֹ:
b'mo'ado hapasakh et Yisra'el v'ney v'ya'asu

Rashi makes the comment: "In its appointed time, even on *Shabbat*; even in a state of impurity"; the latter reinforcing the view of the earlier Sages (*Sifre* 65, *b*. Pesachim 77a) that even when the nation, the *Cohanim* or the implements used are impure, the *Pesach* offering is nevertheless brought in its appointed time: the fourteenth of Aviv (Shemot 12:6) or Nissan in the month names used since the time of the exile in Babylon.

The Preacher, the son of David, who was king in Jerusalem said, "To everything there is a season, and time to every purpose under heaven" (Ecclesiastes 3:1, KJV). The Hebrew text here uses two words: זְמָן, season and עֵת, time; the second of which is used throughout the following seven verses for the repeated "a time to ...". זְמָן is used to refer to the seasons of the biblical feasts, so that *Sukkot* is referred to as זְמָן שִׂמְחָתֵנוּ, *z'man simchatenu*, the time of our rejoicing. Yet neither זְמָן nor עֵת, both of which have the sense of a particular time or season, convey quite the meaning of the word used in our verse: מוֹעֵד, which has a focus not only upon a particular time for an event to occur, but the idea of an appointment: an agreed, scheduled time when two parties will meet to perform some function together or carry out an appointed task.

So we find, at the beginning of the catalogue of the feast cycle in Vayikra 23, that *HaShem* starts by saying: "The Lord's appointed times which you shall proclaim as holy convocations - My appointed times are these ..." (Vayikra 23:2, NASB). The feasts form what a modern Jewish writer called "Sacred Seasons", a cycle of laughing, crying, sharing, rejoicing and remembering before the Lord; a set of physical and spiritual rituals and celebrations to act as a giant mnemonic device for rehearsing and refreshing not only God's goodness to our people in the past but the promise of His continued faithfulness in the years to come, until Yeshua returns and beyond. Carefully arranged, at the natural breaks in the agricultural year, the feasts require our people to step back from work and take time with the Lord; time to relax and remember, time to embrace tradition and commit for the future.

In the same breath as describing the big feasts, the text uses the same word מוֹעֵד to describe the weekly *shabbat* - a day of rest each week, the one day in seven - that is so necessary for our bodies to function and our minds to clear and focus on God. He made us and He knows the exact parameters that our physical bodies work within. If we ignore the Maker's instructions we will wreck the machine; more importantly, when we miss an appointment with God, we miss out on our relationship with Him.

Further Study: Shemot 29:38-46; Matthew 12:1-8

Application: Have you been missing out on your regular time with God; to read and study His word, to spend time talking with Him and sharing times of worship with others? Now would be a good time to reconnect with the inner rhythm that God has put in each of our hearts and meet with Him at the next appointed time.

בְּהַעֲלֹתְךָ ד'

B'ha'alotkha - When you set up - 4

B'Midbar / Numbers 9:15 - 10:10

B'Midbar/Numbers 9:16 So it was always, the cloud was covering it and at night the appearance of fire.

כֵּן יִהְיֶה תָמִיד הֶעָנָן יְכַסֶּנּוּ וּמַרְאֵה־אֵשׁ
eysh oomar'ey y'chasenu he'anan tamiyd yih'yeh keyn

לָיְלָה:
laylah

With verse 15 the narrative of Israel's journeying in the wilderness is rejoined. With the exception of chapters 9 and 10 of Vayikra - the account of Aharon's installation as *Cohen Gadol* and the death of his two eldest sons after bringing strange fire before *HaShem* - these verses might run on directly from the end of Shemot chapter 40. There the *Torah* tells us, "For the cloud of Adonai was above the Tabernacle during the day, and fire was in [the cloud] at night, so that all the house of Israel could see it throughout all their travels" (Shemot 40:38, CJB). Jacob Milgrom describes it as a cloud-encased fire and suggests that "during the day only the cloud is visible, the fire, presumably, dimmed by the sunlight. But night renders the cloud invisible, and the luminous fire can be clearly seen."

This fire is also referred to as 'glory', using the word כָּבֹד, glory or heaviness (Shemot 24:17, 2 Chronicles 7:3, Ezekiel 1:27-28), so that it gives a picture of the glory of God, always present in the midst of the people, but somehow veiled or covered by a sometimes-opaque, sometimes-transparent covering. We can see the proximity and similarity of these two images: the tablets of the testimony contained in the Ark, in the Holy of Holies, seen only by the *Cohen Gadol* and scrupulously covered at all times except during travel when the Tabernacle is dismantled; and the glory of God hidden in the cloud by day but revealed at night, that rises from over the Tabernacle to command the people to move, thus triggering the uncovering of the Ark. In later Israelite history, the Ark was taken to the battlefield to lead the army into battle as a visible sign of God's presence with the armies of Israel (cf. 1 Samuel 4:3-5).

Perhaps this picture is in the back of the gospel writers' minds when they describe Yeshua. John starts the ball rolling with, "The Word became flesh and dwelt among us and we saw His glory ... full of grace and truth" (John 1:14, NASB); the Greek word translated 'dwelt' or 'lived' being close in meaning to 'tabernacled' or "pitched His tent" so that we have the direct reflection of the presence of God in the Tabernacle among His people and the secondary image of the hidden glory of God clothed in human flesh. John continues at the wedding in Cana: "This, the first of Yeshua's miraculous signs, He did at Kanah in the Galil; He manifested His glory, and His talmidim came to trust in Him" (John 2:11, CJB); the cloud thins and the fire within can be seen! As the gospel proceeds we see more signs, revealing who Yeshua is and that phrase is repeated: "This was the second sign that Yeshua did" (John 4:54, CJB). One of the most significant examples comes in the Transfiguration (Mark 9, Matthew 17) where we read that: "As they watched, He began to change form and His clothes became dazzlingly white, whiter than anyone in the world could possibly bleach them" (Mark 9:2-3, CJB). The cloud motif comes a few verses later when, "a cloud enveloped them; and a voice came out of the cloud" (v. 7, CJB) then when the voice has finished speaking, "suddenly when they looked around, they no longer saw anyone with them except Yeshua" (v. 8, CJB). Apart from the stake and the resurrection, the last flash from behind the cloud comes when Yeshua is being arrested in the Garden. Yeshua is approached by the Temple guards, Roman soldiers and some Pharisees; He asks whom they seek and when they reply with His name, He acknowledges who He is by pronouncing the ineffable name. John records, "When He said, 'I AM', they went backwards from Him and fell to the ground" (John 18:6, CJB). Once again, a certain quality in His tone of voice, His authority in claiming His identity, perhaps even a flash of fire in His eyes that John didn't see from behind, and the opacity of the cloud briefly fades to show the glory of God inside.

But is that it? Is it just Yeshua and the pillar of cloud over the *Mishkan*? Luke records that when Stephen was arrested and brought in, "Everyone sitting in the Sanhedrin stared at Stephen and saw that his face looked like the face of an angel" (Acts 6:15, CJB) and at the end of his speech he cried out, "Look! ... I see the Son of Man ... standing at the right hand of God" (Acts 7:56, CJB). We too are to reveal the glory of God that is within us "for it is the God who once said, 'Let light shine out of darkness,' who has made His light shine in our hearts, the light of the knowledge of God's glory in the face of the Messiah Yeshua" (2 Corinthians 4:6, CJB).

Further Study: 2 Corinthians 4:7-10; Daniel 9:17-19

Application: God lives in each of us and wants to be seen by those around us. He is looking for moments when we become transparent enough for Yeshua to shine through. Are you transparent or opaque; are you transparent enough? Why not ask God during this week to clean off the film so that Yeshua in you can be seen again.

בְּהַעֲלֹתְךָ 'ה

B'ha'alotkha - When you set up - 5

B'Midbar / Numbers 10:11 - 34

B'Midbar/Numbers 10:11 the cloud was lifted from over the Tabernacle of the Testimony

נַעֲלָה הֶעָנָן מֵעַל מִשְׁכַּן הָעֵדֻת:

ha'eydut mishkan mey'al he'anan na'alah

This remarkable event - the lifting of the cloud that presaged the move away from Mt. Sinai - is immediately prefaced by a date: "It was in the second year, in the second month, on the twentieth of the month". How long had the Israelites been there? How long was it since they came out of Egypt? Rashi helps us here: "they spent twelve months less ten days at Horeb, for, see now, on the first of the month of Sivan (the third month) they encamped there, and they did not travel until the twentieth of Iyyar (the second month) of the following year." Rashi is working from Moshe's account: "In the third month after the people of Israel had left the land of Egypt, in that day they came to the Sinai desert" (Shemot 19:1).

Sforno tells us something else about the significance of the date: "After those who were unclean had offered the second *Pesach* lamb on the fourteenth day of the month, the trumpets were made with which the congregation and princes were called to Moshe ... and thus the cloud ascended to move forward to Kadesh Barnea." Before the people could move forward, certain things had to be set in place and everything made ready for the journey, the campaign, the entry into the Land. The early chapters of B'Midbar have covered a lot of ground: the census, the banners for the tribes, the purification of the camp, the consecration of the Levites, the dedication of the altar, the offering of both *Pesach* sacrifices and the making of the trumpets. Now Israel was ready to enter the Land. Nechama Leibowitz comments, "Their whole progress in the wilderness was governed by the hand of Divine Providence and they marched forward led by their Heavenly Sovereign: 'At the command of the Lord, the children of Israel journeyed, and at the command of the Lord they pitched' (B'Midbar 9:18)". After all the preparation, Israel moved off, at the pre-arranged time and signal - "they moved out for the first time according to the commandment of the Lord through Moshe" (B'Midbar 10:13, NASB) - a signal that was obvious to all, confirmed by the blowing of the trumpets.

The prophets spoke of many things that were to come, both in their time and ours, as we draw towards the conclusion of days. Some were fulfilled in their lifetimes - Jeremiah's prophecies concerning the capture and destruction of Jerusalem by the Babylonians, for example; some awaited fulfillment until the time of Yeshua, when many prophecies were fulfilled concerning the coming, the death and the resurrection of Messiah. Others, spoken by the prophets before Yeshua's time, by Yeshua Himself and by the New Covenant writers, still look for their fulfillment to the present age or beyond, depending on God's exact timetable. Of one thing we can be certain, however, that the established pattern will be maintained: a time of announcement and preparation so that all should be ready, a clear and unambiguous signal so that all may move forward together in an orderly way, and a significant moving of the people of God that no-one will be able to miss. That sounds very much like the words Yeshua and Rav Sha'ul used to describe the Lord's return, but it is a pattern that has been repeated many times before and will yet be used again at the very end of times.

On three separate occasions within just a few chapters, the prophet Isaiah used the word 'new' in connection with things that God was announcing. "See, the former things have come to pass, and new things I now declare; before they spring forth, I tell you of them" (Isaiah 42:9, NRSV); "Do not remember the former things, or consider the things of old. I am about to do a new thing; now it springs forth, do you not perceive it?" (43:18-19, NRSV); "You have heard; now see all this; and will you not declare it? From this time forward I make you hear new things, hidden things that you have not known" (48:6, NRSV). Notice the time progression, from a context of things having happened and new things yet to be spoken, to one of moving beyond the past and into a future that is just about to happen, finally to a time of using the past as a basis for declaration because new things are now being spoken. Over 2,600 years later, the same patterns are being reworked again as we can see waves and ripples of revival spreading as the Kingdom of God breaks through in our days.

After Peter's inspired confession that Yeshua was the Messiah, the Son of God, at Cæsarea Philippii, the three synoptic gospels all record a change in Yeshua's ministry. "From that time on, Yeshua began making it clear to His talmidim that He had to go to Yerushalayim and endure much suffering at the hands of the elders, the head cohanim and the Torah-teachers; and that He had to be put to death; but that on the third day, He had to be raised to life" (Matthew 16:21, CJB; cf. Mark 8:31, Luke 9:22). Yeshua was preparing the disciples for what was about to happen, even though they didn't understand it at the time, so that when it did come to pass they would recognise it and then later, with the benefit of hindsight, understand why it had to be and use it as the basis for their witness and proclamation of the gospel.

We are living in the end of the prelude to the last days, at a time when even the most orthodox of Jewry can say, "the buttons are all polished and we can hear the footsteps of Messiah in the hall"[1]. Truly God is moving among our people as more and more of the youth in Israel are coming to faith in Messiah and there are outbursts of Holy Spirit power with healing and resurrection happening all over the world from India and the Far East to Florida and South Carolina in the USA. The cloud has lifted from the Tabernacle and is calling God's people to move out. Are you ready?

Further Study: Shemot 40:36-38; Luke 9:28-36

Application: What part can you play in these days to be ready for what God has already started to do? Now is the time to seek His face and lay everything at His feet so that we can all fully participate in the coming of the Kingdom of God.

---

1. Rabbi Joseph Isaac Schneersohn (1880-1950), known as the Previous Rebbe, the 6th in the line of Lubavitch rebbes

בְּהַעֲלֹתְךָ

B'ha'alotkha - When you set up - 6

B'Midbar / Numbers 10:35 - 11:29

B'Midbar/Numbers 10:35 Arise, O Lord, and let Your enemies be scattered and let those who hate You flee before You.

קוּמָה | יהוה וְיָפֻצוּ אֹיְבֶיךָ וְיָנֻסוּ מְשַׂנְאֶיךָ
m'san'eycha v'yanusu oyveycha v'yafutzu Adonai kumah

מִפָּנֶיךָ:
mipaneycha

These are the words that Moshe would say whenever the אָרֹן קֹדֶשׁ - the Ark - would move forward on its journey in the midst of the people of Israel. Although the word קוּמָה is a *Qal* imperative ms form with a paragogic ה from the root קום - to rise or arise - Rashi suggests that it should be translated "Halt, wait" on the grounds that it would be disrespectful of Moshe to tell *HaShem* to start moving, but could ask Him to slow down or wait for the people if He got too far in front of them *Targum Onkelos* changes "Arise" into "Reveal Yourself", partly to remove the anthropomorphic physical action and partly to imply that it is *HaShem's* deeds rather than His presence which would cause His enemies to flee.

Rashi also comments, "Those who hate you: These are those who hate Israel, for whoever hates Israel hates the One who spoke and brought the world into being" and cites Psalm 83:3-4 to show that those who hate God are those who conspire against His people: "Behold, Your enemies make an uproar; and those who hate You have exalted themselves. They make shrewd plans against Your people, and conspire together against Thy treasured ones" (Psalm 83: 2-3, NASB).

This verse and the one that follows it have become part of the standard synagogue liturgy; they are recited whenever the *Torah* scroll is taken out of the Ark or returned to it. Judaism sees the *Torah* scroll as being almost an embodiment of God's presence for His name and His commandments are to be found on every page. Two of the prophets - Micah and Isaiah - spoke of this when they said, "For from Zion will go forth the law, even the word of the

Lord from Jerusalem" (Micah 4:2 and Isaiah 2:3, NASB); these phrases too have become part of the same item of liturgy and are chanted either as the *Torah* is taken out of the Ark or while it is being processed around the synagogue.

While some commentators think of these words being directed at the Ark, Hirsch correctly understands that the words are really directed towards God Himself, for where the *Torah* finds a welcome, there also God is welcome. Hirsch says, "Moshe recognised that this *Torah* from its very entry into the world would have to expect opponents and people who would hate it. Its demands for justice and love are so very much in opposition to the dictates of force and selfishness ... The upkeep of these dictates against the laws of justice and love guarantees the coalition of all the people in power who form a tacitly united front in the world, opponents to the *Torah* who form a barrier to the entry of its influence into the world in general." Here, Hirsch is recognising that wherever the word of God seeks entry, there will be vested interests in the world who will be bound to oppose it, who will gather together for the express purpose of blocking such an entry, who will unite to minimise or eliminate its influence among people.

So it was when Yeshua, Himself the Living *Torah*, came into the world and sought to announce the coming of the Kingdom of God. Just after His birth, when He was taken to the Temple for the "Redemption of the Firstborn" ceremony, it was prophesied that He would arouse opposition: "Shim'on blessed them and said to the child's mother, Miryam, 'This child will cause many in Isra'el to fall and to rise, He will become a sign whom people will speak against'" (Luke 2:34, CJB). Although He was welcomed by many, He was quickly surrounded by opponents, by those who tried to silence Him, as the Gospels make clear: "The P'rushim went out and immediately began plotting with some members of Herod's party how to do away with Him" (Mark 3:6, CJB); "They made plans to arrest Yeshua surreptitiously and have Him put to death" (Matthew 26:4, CJB); "The head cohanim and the whole Sanhedrin looked for some false evidence against Yeshua, so that they might put Him to death" (v. 59, CJB). Yeshua spoke about the inevitable divisions that would come about because of Him and the Gospel when He said, "Those who are not with Me are against Me, and those who do not gather with Me are scattering" (12:30, CJB).

We should recognise that in our world too, the word of God still brings division and opposition. As we proclaim the truth of Yeshua - the cross and resurrection, heaven and hell, the coming judgement - our words force people to take sides, either in or out of alignment with God. Our delivery doesn't much matter, whether we try to be diplomatic or confrontational; the very speaking of the words, the acting out of God's commandments, the difference that our lives show from the standards of the world; all these shout louder than we could ever imagine and compel everyone with whom we come into contact to make a choice. Since people instinctively realise that putting off or avoiding a decision is in fact making a choice to reject, they are often openly hostile because their spiritual position has been challenged and making a choice that they would have preferred to ignore or defer or has been forced upon them against their will. We should not think that it is our eloquence that has provoked the response; it is the Holy Spirit working in our hearers' hearts to convict them of sin and their need to repent. In fact, a little more well-judged mention of hell-fire and brimstone would not go amiss in many circles today!

We should always be ready to obey the promptings of the Spirit and be prepared to open our mouths and quote from Scripture at appropriate moments. Let Moshe's words be our prayer at those time, whether we are the one speaking or one of the group where the conversation is taking place: "Arise, O Lord and let Your enemies be scattered." By praying in this way we amplify and intensify the moment; we are calling on God to confirm His own word, to act in the way that He has told us He acts. This is a prayer that is guaranteed to be heard and although the results are not predictable, something will happen. A tense or explosive situation will be defused, a time of sorrow can be transformed to joy, an argument may be resolved, or a serious discussion may dissolve into laughter. "See, the Word of God is alive! It is at work and is sharper than any double-edged sword - it cuts right through to where soul meets spirit and joints meet marrow, and it is quick to judge the inner reflections and attitudes of the heart" (Hebrews 4:12, CJB)!

Further Study: Isaiah 51:9-11; Psalm 110:1-2; Jeremiah 15:16;
2 Corinthians 4:2

Application: If you are timid about quoting Scripture or speaking out something that the *Ruach HaKodesh* has given you, the time has come to be bold. God's word is needed in our world today and He wants to speak through you. Take a deep breath, pray Moshe's words and speak. Your words - God's words - can and will change the world!

בְּהַעֲלֹתְךָ '7

B'ha'alotkha - When you set up - 7

B'Midbar / Numbers 11:30 - 12:16

B'Midbar/Numbers 12:13 And Moshe cried out to Adonai to say, "God, please, heal her, now."

וַיִּצְעַק מֹשֶׁה אֶל־יהוה לֵאמֹר אֵל נָא רְפָא נָא
na   r'fa   na   Eyl   leymor   Adonai   el   Moshe vayitz'ak

לָהּ׃
lah

    Moshe, Aharon and Miriam have been called out to the Tent of Meeting to deal with a spat between the Israelite leadership. Moshe's brother and sister have been muttering about him behind his back and *HaShem* knows that this must be resolved so that the leadership can stay strong and united. After speaking directly to them, Miriam is afflicted with *tzara'at* as a visible sign of *HaShem's* displeasure, but that creates a problem. Aharon asks Moshe to pray for Miriam, that she may be healed - and surely this is part of the reconciliation process: Moshe must pray for those who have been speaking against him as a sign of forgiveness - but why does the text use the verb וַיִּצְעַק - *Qal*, prefix, 3ms, *vav*-conversive, from the root צָעַק, to cry out, especially for help (Davidson) - at this point rather than one of the speech verbs: speak, ask, or even pray?

    Moshe and Aharon have a problem. Although Miriam has been afflicted with *tzara'at*, she can neither be formally declared a *metzora*, nor formally pronounced clean again, because those ritual functions could only be carried out by a *cohen* - a priest - and there were only three priests: Aharon and his two sons Elazar and Ithamar, all of whom were disqualified from examining her or making the pronouncement because they are close family: brother/sister, nephew/aunt. Unless *HaShem* removes the *tzara'at* now, people will see the affliction, isolate Miriam and wait for a declaration of purity which can never come. Without a divine intervention, Miriam has become locked into an *halachic* no-mans's land with no way to move forward or backward.

Rashi explains that the purpose of this verse is to teach us proper conduct in prayer. Just as "one who asks for something from his fellow man must say two or three words of supplication and afterwards, present his requests", so Moshe precedes his request with the words אֵל נָא - God, please. The particle נָא has two distinct meanings. The first is "please, I pray you" and has a softening effect upon requests and orders, many of which are given using the imperative voice. The second is "now" and has the opposite effect of the first, to sharpen an order by giving an immediate time window to its execution. Here we have the particle twice in the same verse, as part of the supplicatory introduction and as an expression of urgency attached to the request itself.

Jacob Milgrom points out that the structure of Moshe's prayer is a "near perfect introversion", A-B-X-B'-A'. The key word רְפָא, "heal" is the pivotal centre, B and B' are identical (נָא, see above) and A-A' are monosyllables consisting of the same voiced consonant, ל. The structure acts like a funnel or lens to focus attention on the key word and gives the prayer its force; it allows it to be brief - thus avoiding any accusation that Moshe showed favouritism by praying longer for his sister than for other Israelites - while maximising its effectiveness. *HaShem* did, after all, reply immediately and resolve the situation. The *Torah* preserves Moshe's prayer as an example of how to pray and God's intervention to answer his prayer.

By Second Temple times, prayer had often become something of an art form. Formal liturgy was used in the Temple service itself and had been in use in synagogues since the time of the Babylonian Exile. The gospels contain comments about religious people and leaders who would make long prayers in public, sometimes on the street corners, in order to be seen and thought righteous (Matthew 6:5, Mark 12:40). The Jewish writings speak of seven different types of Pharisees, including the *shikmi* Pharisee who performs the actions of Shechem[2] - that is one who carries his religious duties "on his shoulder", that is, ostentatiously (*b.* Sotah 22b). Yeshua Himself warned the disciples not to pray in a long-winded way: "when you are praying, do not use meaningless repetition, as the Gentiles do, for they suppose that they will be heard for their many words" (Matthew 6:7, NASB). The disciples wondered how they were supposed to pray, so after watching for a while, "One time Yeshua was in a certain place praying. As He finished, one of the talmidim said to Him, 'Sir, teach us to pray, just as Yochanan taught his talmidim'" (Luke 11:1, CJB). Yeshua replied with a short and concise template - specimen - that the disciples could use: "He said to them, 'When

---

2. "of Shechem" relates to the men of Shechem who were circumcised in order to be able to marry the household of Ya'akov (B'resheet 34:20-24), so performed a religious action for a public-relations reason.

you pray, say: "Father, May Your name be kept holy. May Your Kingdom come. Give us each day the food we need. Forgive us our sins, for we too forgive everyone who has wronged us. And do not lead us to hard testing"'" (vv. 2-4, CJB).

Yeshua taught the disciples to pray in a direct and straightforward way, knowing that He was also to be the means of the prayer being answered as He is God's intervention to solve our problem with sin. His prayer in the Garden on the night that He was arrested was similarly short; urgent and intense certainly, but short on words: "'Father, if You are willing, take this cup away from Me; still, let not My will but Yours be done' ... in great anguish He prayed more intensely, so that His sweat became like drops of blood falling to the ground" (22:42-44, CJB). Less than twelve hours later, He prayed for those who were crucifying him: "Father, forgive them; they don't understand what they are doing" (23:34, CJB).

So where do we stand today on our prayer and worship life? Liturgy has an important stabilising and levelling function in many churches and congregations, providing comfort and continuity when individual words don't seem adequate, but can become automatic, recited by rote. Spontaneity is valued in other congregations, as a fresh and alive expression of the *Ruach* moving among God's people, but can also drift into automatic or programmed patterns. Are we prepared not only to pray, but to be a part of the answer that God may want to give in response to our prayer? Who are we really praying to or for - to God who hears and responds to every prayer, or for other people around us? Even when we pray for other people, it is important to pray to God and not just to make other people feel better. Short, direct and simple prayers, spoken in faith, offered as part of our covenant relationship with God, are guaranteed an answer. "The effective prayer of a righteous man can accomplish much" (James 5:16, NASB).

Further Study: Psalm 30:2-4(1-3); Jeremiah 17:14; B'resheet 18:23-32

Application: What is your own prayer life like? Do you struggle for words and find it hard to speak frankly and honestly to God? Why not try Moshe's model? Keep it short, polite and to the point. Ask God Himself to help you pray, then watch Him answer that prayer and so many more.

שְׁלַח-לְךָ

Sh'lakh L'cha - Send for yourself

B'Midbar / Numbers 13:1 - 15:41

רִאשׁוֹן	Aliyah One	B'Midbar/Numbers 13:1 - 20
שֵׁנִי	Aliyah Two	B'Midbar/Numbers 13:21 - 14:7
שְׁלִישִׁי	Aliyah Three	B'Midbar/Numbers 14:8 - 25
רְבִיעִי	Aliyah Four	B'Midbar/Numbers 14:26 - 15:7
חֲמִשִׁי	Aliyah Five	B'Midbar/Numbers 15:8 - 16
שִׁשִּׁי	Aliyah Six	B'Midbar/Numbers 15:17 - 26
שְׁבִיעִי	Aliyah Seven	B'Midbar/Numbers 15:27 - 41

שְׁלַח־לְךָ א׳
Sh'lakh L'cha - Send for yourself - 1

B'Midbar / Numbers 13:1 - 20

B'Midbar/Numbers 13:2 Send men on your behalf to reconnoitre the land of Kena'an

שְׁלַח־לְךָ אֲנָשִׁים וְיָתֻרוּ אֶת־אֶרֶץ כְּנַעַן
K'na'an eretz et v'yatooru anashiym l'cha sh'lakh

Rashi devotes many words to commenting in this phrase. He points out that this is not a command that God is giving Moshe; rather that God is permitting Moshe to send men out if the people felt it was necessary, at Moshe's discretion (Devek Tov). He deduces this by comparing this account to that related by Moshe some forty years later: "You approached me, every one of you, and said, 'Let's send men ahead of us to explore the country ...'" (D'varim 1:22, CJB). So we see that the people asked Moshe, and Moshe asked God, and God said, "If you want/need to". The Talmud adds that the very act of asking to send a forward party to investigate the Land was already showing a lack of faith (b. Sotah 34b), for had God not promised "a land flowing with milk and honey" (Shemot 3:17, CJB). From there, one thing led to another; the people received the bad report from the spies and refused to enter the Land, "a good and spacious land, a land flowing with milk and honey" (Shemot 3:8, CJB).

Early in Luke's gospel we read about a certain priest, Zechariah by name, who was visited while burning incense in the Temple, by an angel of the Lord who told him that, "your prayer has been heard. Your wife Elisheva will bear you a son and you are to name him Yochanan" (Luke 1:13, CJB). Only five verses later, as soon as the angel had finished speaking, Zechariah makes the same mistake, "How can I be sure of this? For I am an old man; my wife too is well on in years" (Luke 1:18, CJB) and is bound to silence until the birth of the child as a punishment for his lack of faith.

Thirty or so years later, we find an impulsive fisherman falling for the same problem. Remember how Yeshua had sent the disciples on ahead to cross the lake (the Kinneret) while He sent the crowds away and then caught them up in the middle of the night by walking across the lake to join them? Then Peter calls out to Yeshua, "Lord, if it really is You, tell me to come to You on the water" (Matthew 14:28, CJB). So far, so good, and Yeshua replies, "Come on then!". So Peter gets out of the boat and walks towards Yeshua on the water. But then Peter sees the wind (v. 30) and entirely forgetting that Yeshua had told him to come, he panics, loses faith and starts to sink so that the Master has to grab hold of him (v. 31). Which made Peter feel worse? - starting to sink or Yeshua's rebuke, "O you of little faith, why did you doubt?"

When we have a clear promise and instruction from the Lord, we must persevere over our doubts and push ahead to obey Him in faith, if we don't want soaking wet trousers or, worse, 40 years in the desert.

Further Study: Judges 6:36-40; Romans 5:1-5

Application: When the going gets tough, it is easy to doubt God's call, even if we were certain of it at one time. We start asking other people if God really meant it and trying to re-evaluate the call in the light of our personal circumstances. If this is you, now is the time to stop looking at yourself and to start trusting God and holding on.

שְׁלַח־לְךָ ב'

Sh'lakh L'cha - Send for yourself - 2

B'Midbar / Numbers 13:21 - 14:7

B'Midbar/Numbers 13:21 And they went up and they spied out the land

וַיַּעֲלוּ וַיָּתֻרוּ אֶת־הָאָרֶץ
ha'aretz et vayatooru vaya'alu

Both in the commissioning of the twelve spies and this narrative of them setting out on their mission, the Hebrew word תּוּר is used to describe the purpose of the exercise. Moshe sent the spies, on behalf of the people, to reconnoitre the Land that the Lord was giving them; they went up into the Land and spied it out. But the English translations conceal a wide variety of meaning in the Hebrew that can tell us a lot about how we look at people or events around us.

The basic meaning of the root תּוּר is "to go round or about" - one might almost think it was related to the English word 'tour' which it sounds like! - and from it are derived five different meanings. Firstly, it can mean to go or travel about as a merchant, inspecting the various goods that one might purchase, buying and selling merchandise or produce; a commercial trip or venture. Secondly, the word can be used to mean searching out, exploring or investigating; there is a famous rabbi known as "HaTur" because of his precise *Torah* commentary investigating the hidden connections between the words in the Hebrew Scriptures. Taking it a step further, the third meaning is that used in our text: to go about as a spy, to spy out; now the investigation has become covert and the seekers themselves are to some degree hidden. Another stage on reaches the meaning of to think or purpose, to plan or devise - as seen in Ecclesiastes 2:3. One traditional Orthodox view of the ten spies who returned with a bad report is that they had planned to do so all along (see Tanchuma 5; Sotah 34b). Finally, the last meaning is to go astray astray - as found in the closing verses of this week's *parasha* when the Lord instructs Moshe about the *tzitzit*, fringes, to be worn, "so that you won't go around wherever your own heart and eyes lead you" (B'Midbar 15:39, CJB). What starts out as a simple every-day exercise to buy or sell can be taken so far that it ends in deceit, plotting and going astray.

In the Sermon on the Mount, Yeshua tells the *talmidim*, "If your right eye makes you sin, gouge it out and throw it away! Better that you should lose one part of you than have your whole body thrown into Gei-Hinnom" (Matthew 5:29, CJB). The eye is one of the most amazing organs in the body: not only light sensitive, but able to focus, discern colour and shape, and with a depth of view for detail and scope that it cannot be matched by any man-made device. Yet it is with the eye that we see things that we do not have or that we should not see; the eye can create desire if allowed to freely roam and lead us into sin. As the spies sent out to report on the Land before them should have stayed focussed on their objectives and not allowed themselves to be led into plotting and going astray, so we must govern our eyes and what we see with them.

Further Study: Matthew 6:22-24; Shemot 20:17; Ephesians 5:3-5

Application: It is easy to spend time gazing around, either with the eyes or the mind, day-dreaming and imagining what might be nice to do or to have. Next time you find yourself doing that, compare your thoughts with the word of God on the subject.

שְׁלַח־לְךָ ג'

Sh'lakh L'cha - Send for yourself - 3

B'Midbar / Numbers 14:8 - 25

B'Midbar/Numbers 14:8 If Adonai delights in us, then He will cause us to enter into this land

אִם־חָפֵץ בָּנוּ יהוה וְהֵבִיא אֹתָנוּ אֶל־הָאָרֶץ
ha'aretz el otanu v'heyviy Adonai banu khafeytz im

הַזֹּאת
ha'zot

The verb חָפֵץ is key to Caleb and Joshua's argument with the people over whether Israel should - or could - enter the Land at this point after sending in the twelve spies to reconnoitre the territory ahead of them. Although the *Qal* affix form is most often translated as a past tense, here - particularly coupled with 'if' - it is referring to a state rather than an action, so חָפֵץ should be translated in the present tense. חָפֵץ is also one of a genre of verbs that are connected to their objects by what would be an unusual preposition in English; other verbs in the same genre include 'choose' and 'rebuke' - the effect is not directed at or towards those chosen or rebuked, but is seen as being placed within them. So here: *Adonai's* delight or pleasure is in or within 'us', the people, rather than over or about us. Put another way: *Adonai's* delight is based on who He is and who we are, rather than what we have done.

So, Caleb and Joshua's argument goes: if *Adonai* delights in us, and because He is in complete and absolute control, then it doesn't matter what the obstacles may be, He will bring us into the Land. Notice also the voice of the second verb: while 'bring' is a common translation, here it doesn't do justice to the sense of what is being said. God will cause the Israelites to enter the Land; not just that He will lead them in - although He will do that as well - but that He will make it happen, He will cause the people to enter and take possession of the Land. This cuts completely across the complaints of the other ten spies who talked of giants, being like grasshoppers and that land that devoured its inhabitants; these complaints are not addressed or rebutted in any way because they are simply irrelevant. God, who is bigger than all the possible difficulties will cause the people to enter the Land. Period. Full stop.

Rav Sha'ul takes up the same argument when he writes to the Jewish community in Rome. "What then are we to say to these things? If God is for us, who can be against us?" (Romans 8:31, CJB). To Sha'ul it just isn't possible that God would give us His Son - given up as a sacrifice for us, to redeem us, to restore relationship between man and God - and then allow us to be cut off from Himself again. "Who will separate us from the love of the Messiah? Trouble? Hardship? Persecution? Hunger? Poverty? Danger? War? ... For I am convinced that neither death nor life, neither angels nor other heavenly rulers, neither what exists nor what is coming, neither powers above nor powers below, nor any other created thing, will be able to separate us from the love of God which comes to us through the Messiah Yeshua, our Lord" (Romans 8:35,38-39, CJB).

Further Study: 2 Samuel 22:19-20; Psalm 147:10-11; John 10:27-29

Application: Are you going through a tough patch at the moment, or are you finding it difficult to believe that God can "get there from here"? If so, then you need to hear that argument of Caleb and Joshua. God can and will deliver on every promise He has made and is completely capable of making you enter the land.

שְׁלַח־לְךָ 'ד

Sh'lakh L'cha - Send for yourself - 3

B'Midbar / Numbers 14:26 - 15:7

B'Midbar/Numbers 14:27 Until when [how long] for this evil assembly, that causes complaint against Me?

עַד־מָתַי לָעֵדָה הָרָעָה הַזֹּאת אֲשֶׁר הֵמָּה
heymah asher hazot hara'ah la'eydah matay ad

מַלִּינִים עָלָי
alay maliyniym

    Rashi points out that the participle מַלִּינִים is in the *Hif'il* - causative - voice, so that it has the sense of causing or provoking complaint against God. From this he deduces that the "evil assembly" must be the ten spies who brought the bad report of the Land, so causing the people to disobey God's orders to go up and enter the Land. On that basis, Rashi echoes the words of Rabbi Hiyya that the minimum size of an assembly - in Jewish thought, a *minyan* - is ten men (*b*. Megilah 23b). Although 'assembly' can be - and is, frequently - used for much larger groups, the smallest group that can still be considered representative of the community and be covered by the word 'assembly' is ten. In orthodoxy, the ten must be men, since only men are considered obligated to the time-bound commandments such as praying the prayer services; however, the other streams of Judaism count women as equal partners in the assembly.

    Sforno, translating the last phrase "that keeps murmuring against Me", comments by putting these words in God's mouth: "for they caused others to sin and the sin of the multitude lies with them; hence I shall not practice forbearance with them at all; I have set My face to punish them." The rabbis teach that repentance is always accepted, but that there are times when God does not help us by giving us the spirit of repentance. Perhaps this can most clearly be seen when Isaiah is told, "Render the hearts of this people insensitive, their ears dull and their eyes dim, lest they see with their eyes, hear with their ears, understand with their hearts and return and be healed"

(Isaiah 6:10, NASB). So in this case, Sforno is suggesting that" because the ten spies were continuing to cause the people to sin against God by their incessant complaints, He would withhold repentance from them so that they could not be forgiven. The Sages wrote: "One who influences the masses to sin will not be given the means to achieve repentance" (*m. Pirkei Avot* 5:21), which has at least a ring of Yeshua's words: "And whoever causes one of these little ones who believe to stumble, it would be better for him if, with a heavy millstone hung around his neck, he had been cast into the sea." (Mark 9:42, NASB).

Can this be used as a key to understanding one of Yeshua's most enigmatic sayings? "One can say something against the Son of Man and be forgiven; but whoever keeps speaking against the Ruach HaKodesh will never be forgiven, neither in the olam hazeh or the olam haba" (Matthew 12:32, CJB). What can this possibly mean? If Yeshua is God and the Holy Spirit is God, how can speaking against God be forgiveable, but speaking against God not be forgiveable? Scholars have debated over the centuries what exactly this sin against the Holy Spirit might be and how one avoids committing it.

Yeshua says, "If you ask anything of the Father in My name, He will give it to you" (John 16:23, NRSV) and John writes, "If we confess our sins, He who is faithful and just will forgive us our sins" (1 John 1:9, NRSV). This seems to clearly say that the action of repentance - turning away from sin and asking for forgiveness is a guaranteed process: if we turn to God and seek His forgiveness, we will be forgiven. The Scripture is both clear and unambiguous, and deliberately so - God does not want there to be any doubt. So speaking against Father God, even speaking against Yeshua can all be forgiven once we realise our sin and repent of it; once we acknowledge what we have done or said, experience regret, make amends where possible and appropriate, and ask God to forgive us, He does - every time. But where does that repentance, that conviction of of sin come from in the first place? From our consciences, convicted by the Holy Spirit; that inner voice that tells as that we have done wrong. If we suppress that conviction, then we cannot repent and ask forgiveness, and without asking we do not receive - as simple as that!

Rav Sha'ul warns Timothy about "liars whose own consciences have been burned, as if with a red-hot branding iron" (1 Timothy 4:2, CJB). These are people who not only reject Yeshua, but have set their hearts against hearing the truth from God in any way; they have deliberately shut down the *Ruach HaKodesh* in their lives and so, for them, repentance and consequently forgiveness is impossible - not because God would not grant it, but because they will never ask. May none of us enter that state.

Further Study: Jeremiah 5:20-25; 2 Peter 3:8-9; Acts 3:18-21

Application: Do you find it impossible to go through the day without complaining about something? Things are just never quite right, never the way you would do them? Complaining is cyclic and often draws others into a spiral that we cannot escape without God's intervention. If that is you, then make today the day you cry out to God for repentance and the ability to see and receive His blessings.

שְׁלַח־לְךָ ה'

Sh'lakh L'cha - Send for yourself - 5

B'Midbar / Numbers 15:8 - 16

B'Midbar/Numbers 15:8 And when you shall prepare a son of the herd as a burnt offering or a sacrifice ...

וְכִי־תַעֲשֶׂה בֶן־בָּקָר עֹלָה אוֹ־זָבַח
zavakh o   olah   bakar   ven   ta'aseh v'chiy

    Burnt offerings (see Vayikra 1:2) may be from the flock or the herd; 'flock' means sheep or goats, 'herd' meaning cattle. The previous few verses have been dealing with the accompanying grain and drink offerings for a ram, while this verse moves on to בֶן־בָּקָר, a son of the herd, a young bull. In some instances the choice of which animal to offer is dictated either by the kind of offence, the wealth of the individual or the status of the offering. In other situations, the choice seems to rest more with the person concerned as to how the offering reflects or conveys what they wish to say to *HaShem* through the offering. For example, bringing a ram might suggest that the person is identifying themselves as one of the flock, a sheep approaching or looking up to the Shepherd. Conversely, bringing a bull - both a larger and heavier working animal - may suggest the idea of being a worker in God's kingdom; as oxen are often yoked in pairs, it might even signify an acknowledgement of being a co-worker with God. Sometimes, then, the type of offering that is selected may be intended to portray a particular attitude or message towards God, describing the perspective in which the person sees themselves and their relationship with God.

    A number of the prophets spoke about Israel's attitude to the offerings as an indicator of their attitude and relationship to God. "'You also say, "My, how tiresome it is!" And you disdainfully sniff at it,' says the Lord of hosts, 'and you bring what was taken by robbery, and what is lame or sick; so you bring the offering! Should I receive that from your hand?' says the Lord" (Malachi 1:13, NASB). The priests are being rebuked for their sin in bringing very much less than perfect animals as sacrifices in the Temple. "When you present the blind for sacrifice, is it not evil? And when you present the lame and sick, is it not evil?" (v.8 NASB). The Temple and the ritual service were falling into dishonour because the attitude behind the sacrifices was wrong. Instead of seeking out the best and bringing that to God, the people were sacrificing those animals that they did not want to keep for themselves, passing off the worst of their flocks for sacrifice and so indicating that the commitment to God was in the wrong state. "'Oh that there were one among you who would shut the gates, that you would not uselessly kindle fire on My altar! I am not pleased with you,' says the Lord of hosts, 'nor will I accept an offering from you'" (v.10, NASB). When the attitude is wrong, the whole sacrifice is wrong, the ritual does not 'work' and God cannot accept it.

The Hebrew word תֵעָשֶׂה comes from the root עָשָׂה, a very common verb which is most often translated as "to do, work or make". Here it has the sense of "to make ready, prepare or dress", as of a meal, a feast, a sacrifice (see Davidson and Brown-Driver-Briggs). It speaks of deliberate action to prepare something in advance, following a recipe or a procedure to bring something to the point of readiness, so that it can be sued, offered, eaten or given. Rav Sha'ul clearly has this in view when he writes to the Corinthians about an offering that they were going to make to support the community in Jerusalem: "So I thought it necessary to urge these brothers to go on ahead of me and prepare your promised gift in plenty of time; this way it will be ready when I come and will be a genuine gift, not something extracted by pressure" (2 Corinthians 9:5, CJB). Sha'ul doesn't want to turn up in Corinth and then have to start collecting the money the people had promised, because then people would feel under pressure to give and their attitude would be wrong so the process of giving would not work for them. Sha'ul continues: "Here's the point: he who plants sparingly also harvests sparingly. Each should give according to what he has decided in his heart, not grudgingly or under compulsion, for God loves a cheerful giver" (vv. 6-7, CJB). Whilst we do not give in order to receive, Sha'ul senses God's heart: the attitude to the offering is more important than the value of the offering, because it is the attitude of the heart that God is interested in rather than the money. God, who after all owns "the cattle on a thousand hills" (Psalm 50:10, NASB), can easily arrange for money to be where He knows it needs to be; but He chooses not to command our hearts or demand our offerings - they are to be offered willingly and generously so that they will be a pleasing sacrifice to God, a sweet smelling aroma before Him.

Yeshua spoke in exactly the same terms when He called people to follow Him: "If anyone wants to come after Me, let him say 'No' to himself, take up his execution-stake daily and keep following Me" (Luke 9:23, CJB). There is no compulsion here, no force-majeure to coerce us into reluctant or unwilling submission; this is a frank - for it does not hide the costs involved - invitation to join the Master on His travels, to enter the KLingdom of God willingly, of our own free-will and so to experience true and open relationship with God. So Yeshua echoes the words of the *Torah*: if you want to bring a burnt offering or a sacrifice, then prepare it and come - "Follow Me!"

Further Study: Leviticus 22:17-25; 1 Corinthians 15:58

Application: How do you relate to offerings? Is your life an offering set apart and holy for God? Think about what sort of offering is appropriate to respond to what Yeshua has done for us and how you might prepare it for Him.

שְׁלַח־לְךָ

Sh'lakh L'cha - Send for yourself - 6

B'Midbar / Numbers 15:17 - 26

B'Midbar/Numbers 15:18 When you come to the Land, to which I am bringing you there ...

בְּבֹאֲכֶם אֶל־הָאָרֶץ אֲשֶׁר אֲנִי מֵבִיא אֶתְכֶם
etchem   meyviy   ani   asher   ha'aretz   el   b'vo'achem

שָׁמָּה:
shamah

    The first word of the text, the start of this sequence of words that Moshe was instructed to tell the Sons of Israel, בְּבֹאֲכֶם, is made up of three parts: the tightly coupled preposition בְּ - most often 'in', a *Qal* infinitive from the root בּוֹא - to come or enter, and a 2mp possessive pronoun suffix כֶם - your. It literally means in-your-to-come, but this construction is usually translated by taking the preposition as 'when' and the infinitive as if it were a participle, so "when you come". Rashi immediately comments that this "coming" is different from all the other "comings" in the *Torah* that relate to the Land of Israel. All the others use the particle כִּי - that, for, because, but in this context 'when' - followed by a regular verb form. D'varim 26:1, for example, uses the phrase כִּי־תָבוֹא אֶל־הָאָרֶץ - when you come to or enter the Land - using a 2ms prefix form of the verb referring to the people as one; Vayikra 14:34 has כִּי תָבֹאוּ אֶל־אֶרֶץ כְּנָעַן - when you come to or enter into the Land of Canaan - using a 2mp prefix form of the verb because it is speaking of the separate houses of the individual Israelites.

    Rashi explains that by rabbinic hermeneutical methods[3], conditions that are explicitly stated in one instance of a situation or text also apply in all similar situations. Applying this rule, the instance "When you enter the land which the Lord your God gives you, and you possess it and live in it" (D'varim

---

3. hermeneutics is the study of the theory and practice of interpretation, so these are the methods of interpretation developed and used by the rabbis

17:14, NASB) is used to defer the onset of all the other "when you enter" commands until after not only the entry but also the possession and settlement of the Land had taken place, a further fourteen years after we crossed the Jordan. Because our text above has a different formulation however, and is a command relating to bread which came from the harvest of the Land immediately the people entered, Rashi claims that the Israelites were obligated to separate *challah*[4] from their dough as soon as the people crossed the Jordan, before the settlement and possession of the Land.

Overall, with its focus upon the feasts of the Lord as holy times rather than on the predominance of creating lots of holy space - there was only one Temple - the Bible does seem to express more of a concern about when things are done, rather than where or how they are done (although these are, of course, also important). In the famous passage from the book *Qohelet*, the writer states, "To every thing there is a season, and a time to every purpose under the heaven" (Ecclesiastes 3:1, KJV). After listing major life-cycle events such as birth and death and apparently trivial activities such as gathering and scattering stones, the author concludes, "He has made everything appropriate in its time. He has also set eternity in [man's] heart" (v. 11, NASB). Not only has God designed our lives and the passage of history in specific times and seasons, but He has also given us a sense of the eternal so that we should be aware that there is more than just the arbitrary passage of hours, minutes and seconds, the units of time that demarcate our days. There is also a dimension outside time to which we are connected, even though we cannot directly sense or measure it. We just know in our hearts that it exists and catch glimpses of it now and then as our finite senses detect an intersection between now and the eternal.

Just as the Sages were concerned about when and where certain commandments did or did not apply, so as to be certain of obeying God and yet being able to live a life that was dependent on the world around them, so the New Covenant writers were aware of the tension between the physical and the spiritual. Speaking about His relationship with the Father and when that relationship would apply to His disciples, Yeshua said, "I tell you that whoever hears what I am saying and trusts the One who sent Me has eternal life - that is, he will not come up for judgment but has already crossed over from death to life!" (John 5:24, CJB). Eternal life, He makes clear, starts now; a believer already has eternal life even though the current physical life is still in progress. Although eternal life cannot yet be seen or experienced, it is a spiritual reality. Yeshua says that the transition between death and life has already taken place. We are already citizens of the Kingdom of Heaven, we are already subject to its regulations and we are already enjoying its benefits.

---

4. the tithe portion

Rav Sha'ul brings the whole thing together: "So then, are we to say, 'Let's keep on sinning, so that there can be more grace'? Heaven forbid! How can we, who have died to sin, still live in it? Don't you know that those of us who have been immersed into the Messiah Yeshua have been immersed into His death? Through immersion into His death we were buried with Him; so that just as, through the glory of the Father, the Messiah was raised from the dead, likewise we too might live a new life" (Romans 6:1-4, CJB). Although not physically dead, we have already died and been buried with Messiah and, like Him, we have been raised and are living a new life. We too have relationship with God, know the presence of the *Ruach* in our lives and reap the benefits of His provision for our lives. This makes us liable for the rules of the heavenly kingdom where sin is not an option; we are already obligated to live in a way that pleases Him. Sha'ul encourages us to put that into practice, to make our lives a reality: "So if you were raised along with the Messiah, then seek the things above, where the Messiah is sitting at the right hand of God. Focus your minds on the things above, not on things here on earth. For you have died, and your life is hidden with the Messiah in God" (Colossians 3:1-3, CJB). We have to walk this out, we have to bring heaven to earth in our lives. We have come to the land - the kingdom - where God has brought us and we now have to live in the manner that God requires.

Further Study: Colossians 2:12-13; Romans 8:11; Ephesians 2:5-6

Application: Do you struggle to see a difference between your life now and before you came to faith in Messiah? Is your experience of daily life compatible with the life you would expect to live in the Kingdom of God? Take it up with the King! Find out what He wants to change in your life and then work with Him to bring it about soon.

שְׁלַח-לְךָ ז'

Sh'lakh L'cha - Send for yourself - 7

B'Midbar / Numbers 15:27 - 41

B'Midbar/Numbers 15:29 ... there shall be one instruction for you, for the one who acts unintentionally

תּוֹרָה אַחַת יִהְיֶה לָכֶם לָעֹשֶׂה בִּשְׁגָגָה׃
bishgagah la'oseh lachem yih'yeh akhat torah

    This verse comes in the middle of a block of five verses dealing with people who sin. The first two (27-28) discuss someone who sins inadvertently, using very similar words to Vayikra 4:27-31. The last two (30-31) apply where sin is committed intentionally. This middle verse acts as a pivot, linking the two cases together by the common theme that the same rules being given in the section apply with equal certainty whether the offender - deliberate or accidental - is a native Israelite, one of the Children of Israel, or a stranger or an alien who is simply living within the community of Israel.

    The *ger* - foreign resident, sojourner, alien - occupied the position of "protected stranger" among the people of Israel. In exchange for a certain loyalty to their hosts[5] and being bound by some of their laws[6], they were formally protected against oppression or exploitation. Although they could not own land, so were usually artisans or day-labourers, some did amass considerable wealth so that they might have large households and be the owners of slaves. On the other hand, many were poor and bracketed with the Israelite poor as recipients of welfare such as the gleanings of the orchards, harvesting the corners of the fields (Vayikra 19:9) or the forgotten sheaf (D'varim 24:19).

    The Rabbis held that the *ger* was subject to the negative commands - prohibitive: you shall not ... - but not the positive commands - perfomative: you shall ... - although there are some obvious exceptions. The *ger* is not

---

5. For example, see B'resheet 21:22-24 where Avraham swears an oath not to act falsely against Abimelech, in whose land he was sojourning.
6. See the block of verses leading up to Vayikra 24:22 where a series of both religious and damages laws are made binding upon citizens and non-citizens alike.

obligated to keep the festivals, although he may not work on days of rest; he may voluntarily eat the Passover, but only if circumcised; he may participate in the cult[7], to worship the God of Israel, provided that he follows the same rules as the Israelites. Scholars suggest that this pattern is concerned with maintaining purity in the Land. Both Israel and the *gerim* live in the Land and so must work together to avoid impurity, while Israel alone is God's chosen people so have specific obligations of relationship and conduct before the nations.

At the same time, this command must be seen in context: the injunction for "one law" given here in this block of verses applies to sin committed accidentally or deliberately; it cannot be extended to suggest that all the *Torah* is applicable to either *gerim* or believers in Yeshua. On the contrary, the balance of the *Torah* and the way in which other texts are worded makes it clear that while some commandments have a "whole community" application, the majority of the *Torah's* legislation is a requirement only for Israel although the *gerim* may participate in many other activities unless prohibited. The instructions for dwelling in a *sukkah* during the Feast of Tabernacles, for example, "You shall live in booths for seven days; all the native-born in Israel shall live in booths" (Vayikra 23:42, NASB), is specifically given to native-born Israelites and presumably excludes *gerim* and even proselytes.

On the other hand, it can be seen that *HaShem's* attitude to sin is always consistent, no matter who is responsible or how it is carried out; sin is still sin and always causes a breach of relationship. The Scriptures are adamant that sin is a universal condition; during his prayer at the dedicating of the temple, Solomon says of Israel, "If they sin against you - for there is no one who does not sin ..." (1 Kings 8:46, ESV) and the book of *Qohelet* extends that to all people, "Indeed, there is not a righteous man on earth who continually does good and who never sins" (Ecclesiastes 7:20, NASB). Rav Sha'ul repeats this for a Gentile audience: "for all have sinned and fall short of the glory of God" (Romans 3:23, NIV). Whilst Augustine's 4th century CE formulation of the Doctrine of Original Sin - that every person is actually born or created a sinner - is rightly to be rejected, it is certainly true that every man, woman and child on this earth has an unwavering tendency towards sin and that however well people may learn to control their behaviour as they reach adulthood (or later), there is absolutely no question but that everyone has some events in their past that they know to be wrong and of which they are not proud.

Similarly, *HaShem's* response to sin is always consistent: "If an individual sins by mistake, he is to offer a female goat in its first year as a sin offering. The cohen will make atonement before Adonai for the person who

---

7. that is, the regular ritual of worship

makes a mistake by sinning inadvertently; he will make atonement for him, and he will be forgiven - no matter whether he is a citizen of Isra'el or a foreigner living with them" (B'Midbar 15:27-29, CJB); a sacrifice is required and the priest makes atonement. The act of sacrificing a life makes the sinner aware of the cost of sin, while the blood provides the covering or atonement "For the life of the flesh is in the blood, and I have given it to you on the altar to make atonement for your souls; for it is the blood by reason of the life that makes atonement" (Vayikra 17:11, NASB).

Since the Hurban - the destruction of the Second Temple by the Romans in 70 CE - Judaism has been unable to bring sacrifices for sin; there is no temple, no altar and no ritually pure priesthood. Instead, relying on verses such as "What does the Lord require of you but to do justice, to love kindness, and to walk humbly with your God?" (Micah 6:8, NASB) and "I delight in loyalty rather than sacrifice, and in the knowledge of God rather than burnt offerings" (Hosea 6:6, NASB), the early rabbis reformulated the sin offerings as a combination of repentance, prayer and charity. Repentance is recognising, regretting and turning away from sin; prayer is communicating your sorrow to God and asking for forgiveness; charity is a token sacrifice - usually money - given to the poor, humbling yourself by giving something of substance away to another. The rabbis argue that since God had allowed the temple to be removed, He must have been prepared to accept an alternative to sacrifice in its place. In the 12th century, Maimonedes went as far as teaching that God always thought sacrifice inferior to prayer and philosophical meditation, but allowed it as a temporary concession to the Israelites until He had been able to wean them away from the practices of the other nations.

By contrast, followers of Yeshua have held that He Himself made the one complete sin offering for all time, validating all the blood sacrifices offered by the Israelites and making forgiveness available to all who ask and believe in Him. Yeshua is both the sacrifice and the priest bringing the sacrifice to God, since He offered Himself. Both require faith: in the case of the ancient Israelites, that a simple animal sacrifice would be "enough" to cover their sins and that God would forgive them; for believers in Yeshua, that the atonement made on the cross is really available simply by asking. In both cases, the church and the rabbis insist that true repentance and, if appropriate, suitable restitution should be made. The writer to the Hebrews explains that the blood sacrifices, although providing a covering for sin - until Yeshua came - were only temporary: "For the Law ... can never by the same sacrifices year by year, which they offer continually, make perfect those who draw near. Otherwise, would they not have ceased to be offered, because the worshipers, having once been cleansed, would no longer have had consciousness of sins? But in those sacrifices there is a reminder of sins year by year. For it is impossible for the blood of bulls and goats to take away sins"

(Hebrews 10:1-4, NASB). Instead, Yeshua, "having offered one sacrifice for sins for all time, sat down at the right hand of God, waiting from that time onward until His enemies be made a footstool for His feet. For by one offering He has perfected for all time those who are sanctified" (vv. 12-14, NASB).

In exactly the same way as the *Torah* provided one rule for all who sinned, whether Israelite or *ger* in the Land, now God's salvation in Yeshua - the forgiveness of sins in His name and relationship with God - is available to Jew or Gentile alike; it is the only way to receive forgiveness, as Peter and John explained before the *Sanhedrin*: "And there is salvation in no one else; for there is no other name under heaven that has been given among men, by which we must be saved" (Acts 4:12, NASB). Rav Sha'ul therefore emphasises that the gospel: "is the power of God for salvation to everyone who believes, to the Jew first and also to the Greek" (Romans 1:16, NASB). Just in case anyone missed that, he summarises in the middle of the next chapter, "There will be tribulation and distress for every soul of man who does evil, of the Jew first and also of the Greek, but glory and honor and peace to every man who does good, to the Jew first and also to the Greek. For there is no partiality with God" (2:9-11, NASB).

Further Study: Vayikra 16:29-31; Romans 3:29-30

Application: Where do you stand with regard to your sin? Whether Jew or Gentile, have you accepted God's only solution to the problem? Believe it and accept it - it is there for you. Today!

Korakh - Korah

B'Midbar / Numbers 16:1 - 20:27

רִאשׁוֹן	Aliyah One	B'Midbar/Numbers 16:1 - 13
שֵׁנִי	Aliyah Two	B'Midbar/Numbers 16:14 - 19
שְׁלִישִׁי	Aliyah Three	B'Midbar/Numbers 16:20 - 17:8
רְבִיעִי	Aliyah Four	B'Midbar/Numbers 17:9 - 15
חֲמִשִׁי	Aliyah Five	B'Midbar/Numbers 17:16 - 24
שִׁשִּׁי	Aliyah Six	B'Midbar/Numbers 17:25 - 18:20
שְׁבִיעִי	Aliyah Seven	B'Midbar/Numbers 18:21 - 32

Korakh - Korah - 1

B'Midbar / Numbers 16:1 - 13

B'Midbar/Numbers 16:1 Korah son of Izhar son of Kohath son of Levi separated himself

וַיִּקַּח קֹרַח בֶּן־יִצְהָר בֶּן־קְהָת בֶּן־לֵוִי
Leyvi ben   K'hat ben   Yitz'har ben   Korakh vayikakh

The first word of the text, וַיִּקַּח, comes from the root לָקַח meaning 'to take' and it is a transitive verb - that is, a verb that expects a direct object. Yet as the passage goes on, there is no object. This causes the ancient commentators to deduce that the verb is to be taken reflexively: he took himself. *Targum Onkelos* changes the verb to וְאִתְפְּלֵג, "and he separated himself", reflecting the ancient traditional understanding that Korah drew away from Moshe, Aharon and the rest of the people; that he gathered others about him and followed his own heart rather than the instructions of the God of Israel. In order to justify his position, he sustained a dispute with the leadership that, of course, eventually led to the confrontation that the following verses tell us about.

The prophet Jeremiah tells us that, "the heart is more deceitful than anything else and mortally sick" (Jeremiah 17:9, CJB), to warn us of the dangers of following our hearts rather than God. The heart has always been seen as the seat of the emotions; that part of us that is governed by feelings rather than logic, by blindness rather than sight, by passing infatuation rather than long-term covenant commitment. Our emotions have great power to deceive us: what we want, what we desire, can be very persuasive in leading us to draw false conclusions, to build castles in the air and even to go astray from our covenant with God. Yeshua comments, "For out of the heart come forth wicked thoughts, murder, adultery ... these are what really makes a person unclean" (Matthew 15:19-20, CJB).

So, as believers, are we to write off and ignore the heart and our emotions? Are we to become simply cold, unfeeling slaves, mechanically following the logic of God's commandments? No, of course not! But our hearts and emotions are to become our servants rather than our masters; we are to govern them rather than being governed by them; and all to be governed by the *Ruach HaKodesh*, living in us. David writes, "May [the Lord] grant you your heart's desire" (Psalm 20:5, ESV). God places His desires in our hearts so that He may then fulfill them; as we spend time with God, getting to know Him, we "prove what the will of God is, that which is good and acceptable and perfect" (Romans 12:2, NASB). He shows us "the good way, that we may walk in it and find rest for our souls" (Jeremiah 6:16). As we align our hearts with God, think His thoughts and desire His desires, we find that instead of separating ourselves, we are drawn into closer and closer relationship with Him.

Further Study: D'varim 10:12-16; Psalm 51:12-19(10-17); Luke 6:43-45

Application: Why not check the state and orientation of your heart. Are you aligned with God or have you drawn away to follow your own desires and thoughts? It can get to all of us, so it is always important to check our spiritual compass regularly with God.

Korakh - Korah - 2

B'Midbar / Numbers 16:14 - 19

B'Midbar/Numbers 16:14 Moreover, you have not brought us to a land flowing with milk and honey

אַף לֹא אֶל־אֶרֶץ זָבַת חָלָב וּדְבַשׁ הֲבִיאֹתָנוּ
havi'otanu ood'vash khalav zavat eretz el lo af

How many of us have struggled under that accusation? "You haven't done ..." whatever it is that is wrong at the time. What was it that Moshe had failed to do? "Go, assemble the leaders of Israel. Say to them, 'The Lord God of your ancestors, the God of Avraham, Yitz'khak and Ya'akov, appeared to me. He said, "I have paid close attention to you and have seen what has been done to you in Egypt. I promise I will take you away from your misery in Egypt to the land of the Canaanites, Hittites, Amorites, Perizzites, Hivvites and Jebusites, a land flowing with milk and honey."' The leaders of Israel will listen to you" (Shemot 3:16-18, GWT). You bet they did! Only they didn't, or they forgot. They lost sight of who had given the promise and who was going to deliver on it. When things didn't happen as the people expected, they turned on Moshe and blamed him for not taking them into the Land, although it was their own refusal to obey God that had brought about the problem.

Yeshua made a controversial promise when He was teaching in a synagogue in Capernaum: "Those who eat My flesh and drink My blood have eternal life, and I will bring them back to life on the last day ... The Father who has life sent Me, and I live because of the Father. So those who feed on Me will live because of Me" (John 6:54,57, GWT). The gospel records that this was such a strong claim that many of His disciples could not accept Him as their rabbi any longer and turned away back to their previous lives before meeting Him. This seems such an outrageous claim that many of the disciples bounced off it - they just couldn't believe that Yeshua really was the Messiah or could deliver on that promise.

The response of the twelve, the inner circle of hand-picked *talmidim*, was more instructive. Yeshua offered them a way out: "'Do you want to leave Me too?' Simon Peter answered Yeshua, 'Lord, to what person could we go? Your words give eternal life. Besides, we believe and know that You are the

Holy One of God'" (John 6:67-69, GWT). The twelve had grasped - by revelation, see Matthew 16:17 - who Yeshua was and although they might not understand at this point what Yeshua's words really meant, they knew that they had to trust Him and go along with what He said.

Many people today struggle in their relationship with God because they feel that He has let them down or because they cannot come to terms with who He is and the claims He has on their lives. Often this is a misunderstanding because people fail to listen properly and realise exactly who is making which commitments.

Further Study: John 6:22-69

Application: If there is a situation in your life where you don't understand what God is doing or think that He hasn't done what you expected, today would be a good time to go back and ask Him what He really said and make sure that you heard correctly and have interpreted His promise aright.

Korakh - Korah - 3

B'Midbar / Numbers 16:20 - 17:8

B'Midbar/Numbers 16:21 Separate yourselves from this assembly and I will consume them in a moment.

הִבָּדְלוּ מִתּוֹךְ הָעֵדָה הַזֹּאת וַאֲכַלֶּה אֹתָם
otam va'achaleh ha'zot ha'eydah mitoch hibad'lu

כְּרָגַע:
k'raga

    The immediate thought from this text might be that *HaShem* was calling Moshe and Aharon to stand aside from the rest of the people so that they would be preserved when the rest were destroyed, so that He could start again with just the two of them. Certainly this is what *HaShem* said to Moshe at the incident of the calf: "Now let Me alone, that My anger may burn against them, and that I may destroy them; and I will make of you a great nation" (Shemot 32:10, NASB).

    Further consideration might yield another alternative: that *Adonai* was instructing Moshe and Aharon not to intercede for the people - as Moshe had in the past - in the same manner as Avraham had stood before the Lord on behalf of Sodom. On that occasion, hearing that *Adonai* was about to destroy the city because "the outcry of Sodom and Gomorrah is indeed great, and their sin is exceeding grave" (B'resheet 18:20, NASB), Avraham pleads for the city: "Suppose there are fifty righteous within the city? ... Suppose forty? ... Suppose thirty? ..." (vv. 24,29,30 ff.) so that the Lord eventually agrees to spare the city if ten righteous men can be found.

    The clue, perhaps, can be found in Avraham's opening question: "Will you actually sweep away the righteous with the wicked?" (v. 23, CJB). The *Sforno* comments: "Separate yourselves - so that your merit shall not shield them" and refers to Job 22:30 - "He delivers even the unclean; so if your hands are clean, you will be delivered" (CJB). By their presence among the people, Moshe and Aharon prevented God's anger from destroying the whole assembly. Whilst the protestant Christian church has traditionally been negative about the idea of merit - either of man having any or of its being transferable, except of course in the one case of Yeshua Himself - it is not an idea that is foreign to the Scriptures. Rav Sha'ul writes: "For the unbelieving husband is made holy because of his [believing] wife, and the unbelieving wife is made holy because of her [believing] husband. Otherwise your children would be unclean, but as it is, they are holy" (1 Corinthians 7:14, ESV). While this does not say that anyone becomes a believer without knowing and accepting Yeshua for themselves, it does say that there is a measure of relationship just waiting to be taken up by the unbeliever and that the blessing and provision for believers can and will overspill to include those for whom they are responsible or to whom they are closely linked.

Yeshua told the disciples: "You are the salt of the earth" (Matthew 5:13). Salt is a preservative and was widely used to preserve meat and vegetables for long periods; it also acts as a disinfectant and healing agent. Yeshua is saying that we have that effect in the world and, that like Moshe and Aharon, our presence holds off God's judgement and wrath. Because we are here and live and work among unbelievers, God's righteous anger at sin is held back for this season so that more people may have the time and opportunity to come to know God.

Further Study: D'varim 29:10-13; Romans 11:16

Application: How can you be 'salt' to your community and those around you? Do you preserve and cleanse the company that you keep? Ask God how you can be more effective in simply being there for people and holding back the onslaught of wickedness in the world today.

Korakh - Korah - 4

B'Midbar / Numbers 17:9 - 14

B'Midbar/Numbers 17:10 Remove yourselves from the midst of this assembly and I will consume them.

הֵרֹ֗מּוּ מִתּ֛וֹךְ הָעֵדָ֥ה הַזֹּ֖את וַאֲכַלֶּ֣ה אֹתָ֑ם
otam   va'achaleh   hazot   ha'eydah   mitoch   heyromu

כְּרָ֑גַע
k'raga

Ramban asks an obvious question: is it that God cannot destroy the rest of the assembly, leaving Moshe and Aharon untouched? "No", he replies, clearly God's supernatural powers can distinguish between persons. So why is it that Moshe and Aharon should withdraw themselves from the people so as to avoid the plague? Avraham asked *HaShem*, "Will you indeed sweep away the righteous with the wicked?" (B'resheet 18:23, NASB). The answer from the Bible seems to be - yes, the righteous perish with the wicked unless they leave the community: Lot and his family must leave the plains of Sodom; Noah is given the ark to ride out the flood; the Israelites in Egypt require blood on the door-posts and live in the land of Goshen. Only in the previous chapter, earlier in this episode of rebellion, "[the people] got back from around the dwellings of Korah, Dathan and Abiram" (B'Midbar 16:27, NASB) so that they should not be swallowed up when the earth split open to consume them. Of course, God can spare the innocent but only - as Avraham's negotiations with *HaShem* show us - if He also spares the guilty.

Hirsch sees our text as a personal invitation: "If you wish it, get yourselves up out of them and I will immediately make an end of those masses that rise up against you." On the contrary, he comments, "they threw themselves down on their faces before God; and instead of going away from the people, Aharon places himself between the dying and the living, to make atonement for them." Instead of accepting God's invitation to have those pesky troublemakers cleared out, so soon after the last uprising, Moshe continues to sense God's real heart for the people and instructs Aharon to engage further with the people - standing in their midst to offer incense for their atonement - rather than withdrawing or disengaging. By remaining with the people and interceding for them, not only did Moshe and Aharon please God, but they also proved to the people that the complaints and accusations they had made were unfounded so that the people would be open to the further proof that God was about to offer them.

We see this dichotomy between separation and integration being a struggle for believers through the ages. The great monasteries of past times were places where men withdrew from the world around them in order to live holy lives dedicated to God: regular services, a simple lifestyle, and serving their communities by giving alms, feeding the poor, healing the sick and providing shelter. At the same time as being separate, those religious communities still had a significant level of integration with the people around them, providing what are now sometimes referred to as mercy ministries. The Jewish world did not, as a whole, embrace the ideas of separated religious communities - the Essene sect being perhaps a notable exception - but because of both covert and overt anti-semitism has often been forced to live a segregated life. The modern church suffers from the same effect in a different guise. One church leader recently remarked, "We have problems reaching into the social housing areas. We no sooner get a few people saved, but they change their lifestyles, become 'church' and 'nice' and move out of the area to a better neighbourhood, so that we have to start all over again."

Rav Sha'ul writes: "Through us [God] brings knowledge of Messiah. Everywhere we go, people breathe in the exquisite fragrance. Because of Messiah, we give off a sweet scent rising to God, which is recognised by those on the way of salvation - an aroma redolent with life. But those on the way to destruction treat us more like the stench from a rotting corpse" (2 Corinthians 2:14-16, The Message). How can we be an aroma in peoples' noses unless we are, in that sense, also in their faces? How can we be available for people to talk unless we are there? How will our lives be seen unless we live cheek by jowl with those who do not yet know Yeshua, be that in the Jewish or Gentile world? One of the most noticeable characteristics of Yeshua's ministry was the way He associated with those whom respectable society had rejected, so that the Pharisees asked the disciples, "Why is your Teacher eating with the tax-gathers and sinners?" (Matthew 9:11, NASB). Yeshua replied, "Who needs a doctor: the healthy or the sick? Go figure out what this Scripture means: 'I'm after mercy not religion.' I'm here to invite outsiders, not coddle insiders" (vv. 12-13, The Message).

Further Study: Jeremiah 5:1; Luke 19:9-10

Application: Over the years, have you built your life into a Christian enclave, with a regular round of church/synagogue, house-group and Bible study, so that you hardly ever see anyone else? Have you separated yourself from those you are meant to be reaching and left them to be consumed? This is not how it is meant to be - ask God to show you how He plans to turn the situation around and get you integrated with the people He wants to reach. Then say "Yes"!

Korakh - Korah - 5

B'Midbar / Numbers 17:16 - 20

B'Midbar/Numbers 17:17 And take from them a staff, a staff for a father's house ...

וְקַח מֵאִתָּם מַטֶּה מַטֶּה לְבֵית אָב
av l'veyt mateh mateh mey'itam v'kakh

The vocabulary here seems confusing, since the word מַטֶּה normally refers to a tribe (see, for example, B'Midbar 1:16) yet here it is translated 'staff'. Milgrom points out that "the staff was the official insignia of a tribal chieftain (see B'resheet 49:10)" and should take this meaning here as the term בֵּית אָב - a near synonym - is covering the meaning 'tribe' or "father's house". The dual meaning of מַטֶּה is going to be significant through this story as the dead staff blossoms to life and represents the living tribe of Levi that God is going to use and bless; more, it is only that living tribe that is qualified to serve in the presence of God. Hirsch comments that another meaning for מַטֶּה - branch, bough - is also in view here as the twelve tribes are branches from the stem of Ya'akov and although in many ways similar - chips off the old block - each has its own unique character and properties.

Each day in the *Amidah* we pray, אֶת צֶמַח דָּוִד עַבְדְּךָ מְהֵרָה תַצְמִיחַ - "May You quickly cause to branch the branch of David Your servant", a clear reference to Jeremiah's words: "Behold, days are coming - the declaration of Adonai - and I will raise up for David a righteous branch - צֶמַח צַדִּיק" (Jeremiah 23:5), and, "In those days, at that time, I will cause to branch for David a branch of righteousness - צֶמַח צְדָקָה" (Jeremiah 33:15). HaShem promises to raise up the seed of David to restore justice and righteousness in the Land and among our people. It has been the traditional understanding of Judaism that this branch from the house of David will be none other than Messiah. But who will Messiah be? Who is this son of David? Let's go back to that stanza in the *Amidah*, which ends: בָּרוּךְ אַתָּה יהוה, מַצְמִיחַ קֶרֶן יְשׁוּעָה - "Blessed are You, Lord, who causes the horn of Yeshua (salvation), to branch". Not only does this prayer hint at the name of the Messiah - Yeshua - but we pray three times every day (except *Shabbat*) that God will increase His strength, better His reputation, magnify His position and appeal, particularly among our people.

As the Son of David, Messiah will display the best characteristics of David - the man after God's heart, the man who interceded for his people, the man who stood between the wrath of God and the people, the man who fought for his people, the man who (at his best times) was faithful and obedient to his own detriment - while bringing a new and unique set of characteristics: love, compassion, teaching, authority. This is why David, speaking prophetically, could say: "The Lord says to my Lord: 'Sit at My right hand until I make Your enemies a footstool for Your feet.' The Lord will stretch forth Your strong sceptre from Zion, saying: 'Rule in the midst of Your enemies'" (Psalm 110:1-2, NASB). David recognises that although Messiah will come from his own seed, his descendants, He will nevertheless be that much above David as David was above the lowliest of his subjects - He will be Lord! As a son of David and the Son of God, Messiah will be a chip off both old blocks!

In his book The Divine Conspiracy, Dallas Willard explains that the process of learning to be a disciple of Yeshua is very like the process of being an apprentice. In past days, the apprentice would study, live, eat and sleep in his master's house, learning to be exactly like his master. Success was measured by the similarity of the workmanship; if an expert could not tell the difference between a pair of gloves, shoes, a brooch or ring - whatever the trade or guild - made by the master and the apprentice then the process was complete. Dallas Willard goes on to suggest that this is how we are to be: as indistinguishable as possible from the Master Yeshua. We are learning all the time to sound like Him, to use His words, to do what He would do, to think as He would think; in every way - while retaining our own unique character - to be like Him. As the saying goes: "If it walks like a duck and quacks like a duck ..."; are there enough characteristics of Yeshua visible in us that everyone knows that we belong to Him?

Moshe was told to take a staff from each tribal leader, twelve in all. He was to write the name of Aharon on the staff of the tribe of Levi and the other tribe leaders were to write their own names on their staff. The staff that sprouted would designate the tribe that *HaShem* had chosen to serve Him in the priesthood and the service of the Tabernacle. Only the staff that God restored to life would be kept in God's presence as a memorial for future generations that the matter was God's choice and not Moshe, Aharon or any group of people forming a committee and voting one of themselves to be High Priest. So it is with us; it is only Yeshua's name on us that restores us to life and qualifies us to be in God's presence. As we blossom, bud and bring forth fruit, we declare to the world who we belong to and serve as a witness to all generations that God is still at work among the sons of men; that we too are chips off the Father's block.

Further Study: Jeremiah 23:5-6; Romans 12:1-2

Application: Take a good look at yourself and see where you look like Yeshua. You may find this easier to do with someone else who knows you well and you can examine each other. As you look, be open to God showing you things that He wants to change and areas where He is pleased with your progress. How much do you resemble Yeshua?

Korakh - Korah - 6

B'Midbar / Numbers 17:25 - 18:20

B'Midbar/Numbers 17:25 Return Aharon's staff before the Testimony for safe-keeping as a sign for the rebels ...

הָשֵׁב אֶת־מַטֵּה אַהֲרֹן לִפְנֵי הָעֵדוּת
ha'eydut lifney Aharon matey et hasheyv
לְמִשְׁמֶרֶת לְאוֹת לִבְנֵי־מֶרִי
meri livney l'ot l'mishmeret

    Following on the heels of Korah's rebellion, "the whole community of the people of Israel complained against Moshe and Aharon: 'You have killed Adonai's people!'" (B'Midbar 17:6[8], CJB). *HaShem* initiated the contest of the staffs to show the people who had been chosen for leadership of Israel: a staff was taken for each tribe and placed in the Tent of Meeting overnight to see which one sprouted buds; this would demonstrate which of the tribal leaders was chosen. As the text tells us, "Aharon's staff for the tribe of Levi had budded - it had sprouted not only buds but flowers and ripe almonds as well" (v. 23, CJB). After Moshe has shown the staff to all the people, *HaShem* tells him to take Aharon's staff back into the Tent of Meeting and place it before the Ark of the Testimony to be kept safe - for it would become a part of the Tabernacle furniture, packed and unpacked by the priests and carried by the Levites - for all generations to know that it was *HaShem* who had chosen Aharon and the tribe of Levi; not that they had chosen themselves. The book of Hebrews tells us that the staff was kept in the Ark with the jar of manna and the stone tablets (Hebrews 9:4).

    The commentators differ as to the exact purpose of both the sign itself and the safe-keeping of Aharon's staff. Whereas *Rashi* firmly states: "as a safe-keeping, as a sign: As a remembrance that I chose Aharon the priest and they should no longer complain over the priesthood", *Nachmanides*

---
8. There is a difference between the Hebrew and English chapter and verse numbering in this section of the text. The Hebrew chapter 17 begins at the English 16:36 and they resynchronise at the beginning of chapter 18 in both reckonings.

does not agree. Explaining that the fire falling on Aharon's offerings on the eighth day of the installation of Aharon and his sons as priests had been the sign for the priesthood, the Ramban claims that the budding staff was a sign of *HaShem's* choice of the tribe of Levi as the servants of the Tabernacle and ritual in place of the first-born. Rabbi Samson Raphael Hirsch glosses over this question, focusing instead on the divine choice: "Just as the tablets of Testimony testified to the fact of the Divine origin of the *Torah*, so did the staff of Aharon testify to the Divine origin of the choice" of the priests and Levites. He sees both as explaining God's supreme role - "it was brought home to the minds of the people that the *Torah* came to the people, it did not emanate from them."

Richard Elliott Friedman, a contemporary scholar, has a much shorter time-horizon in view. Commenting to this verse, "Aharon's staff ... is now saved by the ark as a reminder when people will rebel in future", he notes how Moshe is later told to "Take the staff and assemble the congregation" (B'midabr 20:8, ESV) as a specific sign to the people that they are back in the same rebellious condition again when there was no water after Miriam had died. Moshe is to take the staff as both a reminder and a sign of authority and his misuse of that authority at that point causes both himself and Aharon to forego being able to lead the people into the Land.

The writings of the prophets contain references both to signs and sprouting branches. Speaking through Jeremiah, at the start of the Babylonian exile, of the time when He will fulfill His promises to the houses of Israel and Judah, God says, "When those days come, at that time, I will cause to spring up - אַצְמִיחַ - for David a Branch - צֶמַח - of Righteousness. He will do what is just and right in the land. When those days come, Y'hudah will be saved, Yerushalayim will live in safety, and the name given to her will be Adonai our Righteousness" (Jeremiah 33:15-16, CJB). Writing after the remnant have returned to the Land, God picks the theme up again in Zechariah's vision: "Adonai-Tzva'ot says: 'There is coming a man whose name is Tzemach - צֶמַח [Sprout]. He will sprout up - יִצְמָח - from his place and rebuild the temple of Adonai" (Zechariah 6:12, CJB). These texts are reflected in the 'Kingdom of David' stanza of the *Amidah* where we pray: "May the offshoot - צֶמַח - of Your servant David soon flower, and may His pride be raised high by Your salvation, for we wait for your salvation all day. Blessed are You, Lord - מַצְמִיחַ קֶרֶן יְשׁוּעָה - who causes the horn [strength, reputation] of Your salvation to flourish [sprout]" (Authorised Daily Prayer).

God also spoke about the way in which the people from the nations would receive the light of His relevation: "In the past the land of Z'vulun and the land of Naftali were regarded lightly; but in the future he will honor the way to the lake, beyond the Yarden, Galil-of-the-Goyim. The people living in darkness have seen a great light; upon those living in the land that lies in the shadow of death, light has dawned" (Isaiah 8:23-9:1, CJB), quoted in Matthews gospel (Matthew 4:15-16). Yeshua started His ministry in the area of the Galil, an area where many of the nations had come to live since the Assyrian conquest and in Roman times. Yeshua said, "as Moshe lifted up the serpent in the wilderness, even so must the Son of Man be lifted up ... And I, if I be lifted up from the earth, will draw all men to Myself" (John 3:14, 12:32, NASB), referring to His death and connecting it to the bronze serpent that Moshe was instructed to fashion and hold up in the middle of the Israelite camp in the wilderness when there was a plague of snakes (B'Midbar 21:9). Unlike Moshe, Yeshua did not misuse His authority and only did exactly what He saw the Father doing and so completed His mission perfectly. Although widely misused by the church authorities in the past, the cross is God's staff or sign of authority bringing freedom for all who will turn to Him.

Yeshua is the Branch from the root of David. In these days and among our own Jewish people, God is answering our prayers and causing the name and reputation of Yeshua - God's salvation for which we have been waiting - to flourish. Every day, more and more Jewish people are discovering the secret that Yeshua is the Jewish Messiah and that to trust in Him is a uniquely Jewish thing to do. As they do and prove by a continuing Jewish lifestyle that they are still Jewish, God is building the believing remnant in our generation who will cry out, "Baruch ha'ba b'shem *Adonai* - Blessed is He who comes in the name of the Lord" so that Yeshua may soon return to take His rightful place as the King of Israel in Jerusalem!

Further Study: Isaiah 60:1-5; John 8:28

Application: If you are Jewish and are struggling with who Yeshua is, be encouraged that the words of Scripture are true and never lie. God has sent His salvation to save His people as He said that He would. You can know that salvation today; all you have to do is ask: Yeshua is His name!

Korakh - Korah - 7

B'Midbar / Numbers 18:21 - 32

B'Midbar/Numbers 18:21 And to the sons of Levi, behold, I have given all the tithe in Israel, for an inheritance, an exchange of their work

וְלִבְנֵי לֵוִי הִנֵּה נָתַתִּי כָּל־מַעֲשֵׂר בְּיִשְׂרָאֵל
b'Yisra'el ma'aseyr kol natatiy hineyh Leyviy v'livney
לְנַחֲלָה חֵלֶף עֲבֹדָתָם
avodatam kheylef l'nakhalah

    In the ancient Israelite economy, the tribe of Levi had no ancestral land inheritance. Instead, as highlighted in our text, the Levites were given all the tithes of the land and served *HaShem* and the people in the role of religious functionaries. The work included direct service as singers, door-keepers and so on at the Temple in Jerusalem, but also covered instructing the people as a whole about the *Torah* and maintaining the cities of refuge positioned throughout the Land of Israel. The Levites could own property in the cities of refuge - houses and fields - and could buy and sell other property subject to the Jubilee year remission/return, and the normal rules of inheritance between one generation and the next applied to all of these classes of ownership. Unlike the other tribes, though, the Levites had no ancestral land holdings - property or farms - that belonged to their families and which would return to them in the year of Jubilee, no freehold right of ownership. Their role was not to be that of farmers and business people, devoting their lives to providing for their families and generating an income; they were to serve *HaShem* on behalf of the people, to minister in the Temple and teach the people about *HaShem*. The *Torah* therefore sets up a support system that provides them with an income and food, so that they can concentrate on their calling before God without needing to be concerned about their livelihood.

    The word חֵלֶף is used here either as a preposition: "in exchange for", or as a noun starting a construct chain: "an exchange of". The word is found in Aramaic and Phoenecian texts with the meaning "substitute", or "compensation". Rabbi Hirsch sees this provision as wages for work done by the Levites, rather than the portion of the offerings brought to God that are eaten by the priests. Indeed, the Levites themselves are required to give a tithe from their tithe income to the priests. Israel Drazin points out that if this were just a proportional business share in the produce of the land, then one tribe in twelve/thirteen[9] should receive only eight percent of the produce, perhaps reduced further because the Levites made no capital investment or labour in cultivation. The tithe is therefore "not to be considered as a share, but as a gift in return for their service."

Most telling, perhaps, is the origin of the institution. This verse comes from a block of instructions given directly to Aharon by *HaShem* Himself that starts at verse 8 in this chapter of the text. *HaShem* says נָתַתִּי - a *Qal* 1cs affix form from the root נָתַן - "I have given" the tithe to the Levites. While the most frequent meaning of the verb is "to give" it is often used in the sense of "appoint, set", so here it establishes the tithe not just as a gift but a divinely appointed wage or regular payment. By giving the instruction to Aharon, one of the relatively few occasions when Aharon is directly addressed rather than being told what to do through Moshe, *HaShem* makes it his responsibility to ensure that it is carried out in the proper manner; the provision for the Levites is just as important a part of the function of the priesthood as the bringing of the sacrifices in the Temple.

There is a tension too between the doing of the work and the provision of the tithe. The Levites are always on duty: seven days a week, throughout the whole year, feasts, *shabbat* and ordinary days; the gates and doors always need attendance, the singers are always needed, the infrastructure and physical cleaning and upkeep of the Temple has to be done, the treasury has to be open and the supplies and provisions of the daily sacrifices must be on hand. The service of the Temple, in its regular cycle of worship to God, must not be interrupted. Notice also that the Temple service continues every year, even in sabbatical or jubilee years, when there was no formal harvesting and agricultural work. The Levites are as dependent upon the provision in the seventh year as the people who farm the land and give the tithe. The obligation upon the Levites to perform this work is not conditioned upon the giving of the tithe - the work must always be done because that is their job. At the same time, the people are to provide the tithe and the priests are to make sure that it is brought in, so that the Levites can be paid for their work.

We know from the biblical and archaeological record that Israel was far from consistent in this respect. At times of religious revival, the tithe was brought in and the Temple ran properly; at other times, little or no produce was supplied and the Levites were forced to go back to their cities and try to

---

9. depending on whether the two sons of Joseph are counted as one or two tribes

eke out a living by working. King Hezekiah "commanded the people who lived in Jerusalem to give the portion due to the priests and the Levites, that they might devote themselves to the law of the Lord. And as soon as the order spread, the sons of Israel provided in abundance the first fruits of grain, new wine, oil, honey, and of all the produce of the field; and they brought in abundantly the tithe of all" (2 Chronicles 31:4-5, NASB), while during the time of Nehemiah, he "discovered that the portions of the Levites had not been contributed, and that the Levites and the singers who performed the temple service had made off, each to his fields. I censured the prefects, saying, 'How is it that the House of God has been neglected?' Then I recalled the Levites and installed them again in their posts; and all Judah brought the tithes of grain, wine, and oil into the treasuries" (Nehemiah 13:10-12, JPS). What was a Levite to do? He had to support his wife and children, put bread on the table for them to eat and maintain a roof over their heads; if his tour of duty in Jerusalem meant that the family would starve while he was away, because there were no tithes, then the pressure to simply stay at home was significant.

In these days of professional clergy, where the rabbi or minister receives a salary for his work in serving the congregation, similar tensions still exist. On the one hand, ministry can become like any other job, where clergy move from position to position to better their income, to work with larger congregations or receive promotion in a hierarchy. On the other hand, ministry can expose clergy to real hardship or abuse where a congregation or board take advantage of a family or an individual who feels called to stay in a situation without proper payment, housing or support. Part-time clergy often combine serving a congregation without payment or on a low stipend, with a standard job in the secular world to generate their main income. Many elders, house-group leaders and others serve in entirely lay capacities, giving hours of their time and often much of their own money, while holding down full-time jobs to support their families.

Rav Sha'ul applies the *Torah* to this issue when he tells Timothy that "The leaders who lead well should be considered worthy of double honor, especially those working hard at communicating the Word and at teaching. For the Tanakh says, 'You are not to muzzle an ox when it is treading out the grain,' in other words, 'The worker deserves his wages'" (1 Timothy 5:17-18, CJB). Quoting the same verse, he also told the Corinthians that "it is written in the Law of Moshe, 'You shall not muzzle an ox when it treads out the grain.' Is it for oxen that God is concerned? Does he not speak entirely for our sake? It was written for our sake, because the ploughman should plough in hope and the thresher thresh in hope of sharing in the crop" (1 Corinthians 9:9-10, ESV), concluding that although he personally was not doing so, "the Lord directed those who proclaim the gospel to get their living from the gospel" (v. 14, NASB).

Whether the tithe - either as a specific or minimum figure - remains a biblical principle that is incumbent upon both Jew and Gentile in the Body of Messiah today is a much debated point. What is certain is that some form of giving, from a personal desire to thank or bless a minister of the gospel (in the broadest sense), from being a committed part of a community supporting its work, or in long term support of individual workers or missionaries, is a significant and commanded part of our walk with the Lord. By regular giving to a local church or congregation we demonstrate our commitment to its vision and values and participate in its calling and mission. By supporting individual workers on a long term basis we develop relationship and stamina both in them and ourselves, working together to grow the kingdom of God. By blessing others who have blessed us, on a spontaneous basis, we show love and appreciation at a personal level that helps and encourages everyone to feel acknowledged and valuable.

Further Study: Matthew 10:9-11; Galatians 6:6; Romans 16:1-2

Application: How can you show your appreciation and commitment within the family of God today? Your action - be that a gift of money, lending a hand, a smile and a word of encouragement, a note by post or e-mail - can lift someone's soul and make their day. Why not ask the Lord who He wants you to bless next.

חֻקַּת

Hukkat - Statute

This portion is sometimes read with the following portion - *Balak* - so some of the following portions are for the joint text.

B'Midbar / Numbers 19:1 - 22:1

רִאשׁוֹן	Aliyah One	B'Midbar/Numbers 19:1 - 17
שֵׁנִי	Aliyah Two	B'Midbar/Numbers 19:18 - 20:6
שְׁלִישִׁי	Aliyah Three	B'Midbar/Numbers 20:22 - 21:5
רְבִיעִי	Aliyah Four	B'Midbar/Numbers 20:14 - 21
חֲמִשִׁי	Aliyah Five	B'Midbar/Numbers 20:22 - 21:5
שִׁשִּׁי	Aliyah Six	B'Midbar/Numbers 22:39 - 23:26
שְׁבִיעִי	Aliyah Seven	B'Midbar/Numbers 21:21 - 22:1

Hukkat - Statute - 1

B'Midbar / Numbers 19:1 - 17

B'Midbar/Numbers 19:2 This is the statute of the Torah, which Adonai has commanded

זֹאת חֻקַּת הַתּוֹרָה אֲשֶׁר־צִוָּה יהוה
Adonai   tzivah   asher   ha'torah   hukkat   zot

    These words introduce the strange ritual of the red heifer; strange because it seems contradictory: it purifies yet renders impure, it cleanses from contact with the dead, yet is itself a product of death. It is a commandment that commentators throughout the years have wrestled with in order to try and unravel its curious paradox - we are still no nearer reconciling the apparent conflict. We fall back on the fact that it is a command of God and so to be obeyed anyway, even without a detailed understanding.

    Rashi points out that it is the custom of the Accuser and the world to provoke Israel by asking questions such as "What is this commandment?" or "What reason is there to it?" in order to shake us in our belief in, obedience to and reliance upon God's word. The enemy's success in the Garden of Eden hinged upon his question to Eve, "Did God really say, 'You are not to eat from any tree in the garden?'" (B'resheet 3:1, CJB). Likewise, Satan questions God when he says, "Is it for nothing that Job fears God? You've put a protective hedge around him …" (Job 1:9-10, CJB). In the early part of the gospel story we find Yeshua being questioned and tempted by the enemy: "If you are the Son of God, command these stones to become bread" (Matthew 4:3, NASB) and "If you are the Son of God, throw yourself down [from the temple]" (v. 6, NASB).

    It is a constant technique of the enemy to question and challenge our faith in what God has said to us: to vary or alter the meaning of the words of Scripture; to weaken or dilute the strength of God's commandments; to move or disturb the boundaries that God has set; to use such politically correct concepts as tolerance, compassion and equality to set aside the simple plain reading of the Bible; to erode and undermine the foundations of our faith; to ridicule and bring into disrepute God's standards for our behaviour and conduct.

And yet, the devil is a defeated foe and God has already declared us the victors in Messiah Yeshua; He has already given us the weapons and authority to overcome the enemy's lies and questions. In the story of Job, we read that the Adversary could do nothing without God's permission and was limited to the boundaries that God set. In the gospels, we read that Yeshua answered the Tempter with the word of God and he was forced to leave, defeated. Peter tells us, "Resist him [the devil], firm in your faith" (1 Peter 5:9, NASB) and James adds, "Resist the devil and he will flee from you" (James 4:7, NASB). The command is clear and the outcome guaranteed.

Further Study: 2 Corinthians 10:5; Matthew 16:13-18

Application: With the command to resist comes the authority to execute the command. Today is a day to shout to the world, "This is the statue of the Torah, which Adonai commanded!" and seeing the enemy melt away before you.

Hukkat - Statute - 2

B'Midbar / Numbers 19:18 - 20:6

B'Midbar/Numbers 19:18 A pure man shall take hyssop and dip it in the water and sprinkle on the tent

וְלָקַח אֵזוֹב וְטָבַל בַּמַּיִם אִישׁ טָהוֹר
tahor   iysh   bamayim   v'taval   eyzov   v'lakakh

וְהִזָּה עַל־הָאֹהֶל
ha'ohel   al   v'hizah

    These instructions form part of the enigmatic ritual of the red heifer whereby a person who has become ritually impure because of contact with a dead body is sprinkled with the water of lustration; but the person who does the sprinkling becomes impure until evening after washing his clothes. Now the process at this particular point specifies אִישׁ טָהוֹר, a pure man, without explicitly saying what that means. Clearly, from the context, it has to be someone other than the person who has become impure - they cannot sprinkle themselves - and it must be someone who is ritually pure.

    The Psalmist gives us more information about the state of those who can approach and serve God. "Who may go up to the mountain of Adonai? And who may rise up in the place of His holiness? The one having clean hands and a pure heart" (Psalm 24:3-4). In the psalm, the word used for clean, נָקִי, carries overtones of 'innocent, free from guilt' and the classic interpretation - in both the Jewish and Christian traditions - is of a person who has been honest and upright, whose hands are free of blood and dishonest gain. Similarly, בַּר, the word for pure comes from a root verb meaning to separate, and is considered to refer to moral purity. Later on, David writes, "Create for me a pure heart, O God" (Psalm 51:12), with the words לֵב טָהוֹר, pure heart, matching the phrase in our text from the *parasha*. Here the implication is that only God can create - or in David's particular case, recreate - the ritual purity, rightness of heart within a man. Written after God had rebuked David for his sin with Bathsheba through Nathan the prophet, the whole psalm cries out to God for forgiveness, reconciliation and re-creation, recognising that only God can do that restoration.

Mark's gospel records one of the moments of challenge between Yeshua and the *P'rushim* in chapter 7, where Yeshua's *talmidim* had been eating their bread without first having washed their hands (see Mishnah Yadayim 2:1). Yeshua responds to the multitudes who had witnessed this challenge, "there is nothing outside the man which going into him can defile him; but the things that proceed out of the man are what defile the man" (Mark 7:15, NASB). The disciples question Him about this, so He goes on to say, "For from within, out of the heart of man, proceed the evil thoughts, fornications, thefts, murders, adulteries ..." (v. 21, NASB). It isn't that Yeshua doesn't care either about hygiene or sensible ritual that focuses upon God and His provision for us, but that He is trying to point out that purity isn't simply an external affair - it is more importantly a question of the state of a man's heart - and to be pure before God, that must have been re-created and restored by God. Without that, what may appear to be good behaviour on the outside may be just that: on the outside.

Further Study: Isaiah 29:13-16; Luke 11:37-41

Application: How righteous are we before God and before men? Is there a difference between the inside and the outside? To be able to serve God, we need to be a pure man with a pure heart - cleansed and set in order by Him.

חֻקַּת / בָּלָק ג׳

Hukkat - Statute / Balak - Balak - 3

B'Midbar / Numbers 20:22 - 21:5

B'Midbar/Numbers 20:22 and the Children of Israel, the whole assembly, came to Mount Hor.

וַיָּבֹאוּ בְנֵי־יִשְׂרָאֵל כָּל־הָעֵדָה הֹר הָהָר:
ha'har Hor ha'eydah kol Isra'el v'ney vayavo'u

Forty years have passed and our people are now on their way back towards the Land for the next generation to enter and take possession of the inheritance that *Adonai* had already given us. The word for 'assembly', עֵדָה, comes from the root יָעַד which means 'to appoint' and is also the root for the word מוֹעֵד which means 'an appointed time - the word used for the feasts and festivals - or an appointment or meeting. It conveys the idea that the assembly - or congregation - has an 'appointed' quality about it, rather than just being a natural or haphazard collection of people. An appropriate term for the group that were not only God's chosen people but the chosen generation to enter the Land.

Rashi comments: "The entire assembly - all of them, whole and ready to enter the Land" and goes on to point out that there was no-one there who was to have died in the wilderness, and that no-one had died in the wilderness who was meant to be there, for this generation was the one to whom God said: "you who stuck with Adonai your God are still alive today, every one of you" (D'varim 4:4, CJB). God had not been indiscriminate or careless during the time in the wilderness; the Lord, the giver of life and the bringer of death, the one of whom we say *Dayan Emet* - the True Judge - knew each of the people and their hearts and His judgement was precisely meted out with absolute justice and righteousness.

As part of the briefing that He gave the *talmidim* before sending them out to heal the sick and proclaim the gospel of the Kingdom throughout the Galil, Yeshua told His disciples: "Aren't sparrows sold for next to nothing, two for an assarion? Yet not one of them will fall to the ground without your Father's consent. As for you, every hair on your head has been counted. So do not be afraid, you are worth more than many sparrows" (Matthew 10:29, CJB).

Not one sparrow - those common little birds that chirp and shout in the hedges, that fight and squawk with each other in the dust baths in the village streets - not one of those will die or fall to the ground without our Father giving His consent and being aware of the situation. If God is concerned even for the sparrows, says Yeshua, how much more will He be concerned about each of the disciples, about each of us.

This is the assurance that enabled Rav Sha'ul, even though he was confined to prison on account of preaching the gospel faithfully, to write: "I am not ashamed, because I know Him in whom I have put my trust, and I am persuaded that He can keep safe until that Day what He has entrusted to me" (2 Timothy 1:12, CJB). Sha'ul knew that whatever befell him, whatever circumstances - not matter how dire they appeared - God was in control and nothing would happen that God did not specifically allow and know to be the best.

Further Study: Psalm 143:6-11; Luke 21:10-19

Application: When the going gets tough, many people despair and conclude that God has abandoned or forgotten them. Far from it - God is still intimately involved in their lives. If this is the way you are feeling today, take heart and know that you are worth more than many sparrows.

Hukkat - Statute - 4

B'Midbar / Numbers 20:14 - 21

B'Midbar/Numbers 20:14 And Moshe sent messengers ... "Thus says your brother Israel ..."

וַיִּשְׁלַח מֹשֶׁה מַלְאָכִים ... כֹּה אָמַר אָחִיךָ
Moshe vayishlakh   mal'achiym   ...   koh   amar   akhiycha

יִשְׂרָאֵל
Yisra'el

    The use of the words וַיִּשְׁלַח מַלְאָכִים, "he sent messengers", seems to be a deliberate reflection of a previous encounter between Israel and Edom in the persons of their forebears Ya'akov and Esav, for the *Torah* uses the exact same words in the narration of that meeting: "And Ya'akov sent messengers before him to his brother Esav in the land of Seir, the field of Edom" (B'resheet 32:4). Both here and on the previous occasion, Ya'akov/Israel are returning to their homeland and have to try and negotiate passage past the potentially hostile Esav/Edom. Hence the sending of messengers in advance and the use of the word אָחִיךָ, "your brother" inviting the Edomites to remember the familial connection and receive the diplomatic request favourably. We should notice the similarities and differences in the two narratives: in B'resheet, Esav approaches Ya'akov with an armed force, but after Ya'akov's gifts and humility, Esav forgives him and shows considerable fraternal affection; in B'Midbar, although Israel makes overtures of peace, the Edomites approach with an armed force and show no sign of forgiveness or affection.

    Moshe's approach to the king of Edom demonstrates an important principle, however. The offer that Israel made to the Edomites was considerable: although they were undeniably a considerable number of people - probably somewhere between two and three million, plus flocks and herds - they offered to keep only to the King's Highway, a well-known and established caravan route used by all the traders who passed through Edom; moreover, although God normally provided both their food and drink, by way of the manna and the well that followed them, they offered to buy all their food and drink from the Edomite merchants, thus providing a considerable boost to the local economy and national economy. Moshe had anticipated that Edom might feel threatened by the presence of Israel and respond in an aggressive way, so he made a conciliatory approach, designed to show peaceful intent, to try and reach a peaceful agreement for Israel's passage through the Land of Edom without the need for conflict.

The writer of the Proverbs tells us that, "A soft answer turns away wrath, but a harsh word stirs up anger" (Proverbs 15:1, ESV) or, as another version says, "A gentle answer will calm a person's anger, but an unkind answer will cause more anger" (NCV). When we respond gently to a person's aggression, rather than in a brusque or abrasive manner, we greatly increase the prospect of being able to reach an amicable or negotiated settlement, rather than having to fight about the issues involved. Do notice, however, that this is not an instruction to surrender your principles or engage in appeasement, simply buying someone's apparent goodwill by giving them what they were demanding - that simply encourages aggression and shows weakness that has historically always led to disaster.

The principle of avoiding conflict at a personal level - while recognising that it may be essential *in extremis* or on behalf of those for whom one is responsible - is one that Yeshua and the apostles took seriously. Yeshua taught, "Make friends quickly with your opponent at law while you are with him on the way, in order that your opponent may not deliver you to the judge ..." (Matthew 5:25, NASB), to show that we should try to reach agreement with people rather than calling for outside arbitration. Acknowledging that it will not always work, Rav Sha'ul comments, "If possible, and to the extent that it depends on you, live in peace with all people" (Romans 12:18, CJB), putting great responsibility on believers to show restraint and not be the ones who escalate a dispute. Rather, we should always seek to reach a peaceable solution to any disagreements that spring up, so that we become known as the people of peace.

Further Study: Isaiah 55:6-7; Job 22:21-22; Hebrews 12:14

Application: Do you find it easy to get along with people, easily turning aside or ignoring potentially critical comments and remarks? Or do you find your hackles rising when people seem to casually pass judgement on your speech, clothes or behaviour? Pray for peace inside and peace to share with those around you in your life today.

חֻקַּת ה'

Hukkat - Statute - 5

B'Midbar / Numbers 20:22 - 21:5

B'Midbar/Numbers 20:24 Aharon will be gathered to his people, for he will not enter the Land

יֵאָסֵף אַהֲרֹן אֶל־עַמָּיו כִּי לֹא יָבֹא אֶל־הָאָרֶץ
ha'aretz el yavo lo kiy amayv el Aharon yey'aseyf

At first sight, this week's text starts with a well-known and common euphemism for dying - he will be gathered to his people, יֵאָסֵף אֶל־עַמָּיו. *HaShem* was telling Moshe that Aharon was about to die. The verb here is a *Niphal* 3ms prefix form from the root אָסַף, to collect together or to assemble, followed by the preposition אֶל to designate the person or place of gathering. Significantly, in two ways, the text carries more meaning than simply that Aharon was about to die, although that is true. Firstly, this idiom is only found in the *Torah* itself, only with the deaths of Avraham (B'resheet 25:8), Ishmael (B'resheet 25:17), Yitz'khak (B'resheet 35:29), Ya'akov (B'resheet 49:29,33), Moshe (B'Midbar 27:13, 31:2; D'varim 32:50) and Aharon (here and D'varim 32:50); it is used only for Israel's forefathers - not for women or non-Israelites - just for the key figures among the patriarchs. Secondly, as Jacob Milgrom points out, "It is the act that takes place after dying but before burial. Thus it can neither mean to die nor to be buried in the family tomb. Rather it means 'be re-united with ones ancestors' and refers to the after-life in She'ol". Consequently, the opposite expression וְנִכְרְתָה מֵעַמֶּיהָ - he shall be cut off from his people (for example Shemot 30:33) - means that a person has been excluded from the afterlife, a punishment that can only be carried out by God.

Some suggest that the concept of an after-life, the עוֹלָם הַבָּא - the world to come - and the idea of a resurrection after death were unknown in "early" Judaism, as if Avraham and Moshe saw their existence in terms of this physical life alone, terminating at death. To be fair, the *Torah* contains little direct information about eschatology, lacking the grand view that Isaiah was granted: "For behold, I create new heavens and a new earth, and the former things shall not be remembered or come to mind" (Isaiah 65:17, NASB), Ezekiel's vision of the dry bones: "Behold, I will open your graves and cause you to come up out of your graves, My people; and I will bring you into the Land of Israel" (Ezekiel 37:12, NASB), or Daniel's startling insight: "And many of those who sleep in the dust of the earth will awake, these to everlasting life, but the others to disgrace and everlasting contempt" (Daniel 12:2, NASB). Nevertheless, this phrase - being gathered to one's people - is a sign that the continuity of life after death was an accepted everyday part of faith from earliest times. Within the writings of every society, some things were so commonplace that they are simply taken for granted and never directly mentioned precisely because everyone knows and accepts them as part of life; our text, and its opposite, provide a sideways glimpse at this certainty of the ancients.

Commenting on the *Torah's* first use of this phrase (B'resheet 25:8), Hirsch says, "Moreover the word אָסַף designates receiving a straying into sheltering protection, and an expelled one back into his original home. According to this, we regard the next world as the real home to which mankind belongs and this world, the testing years of wandering abroad, out of which at the end of wandering, the soul returns home and is received in the waiting circle of those to whom it belongs." Yeshua stands firmly in this tradition when He rebukes the Sadducees for their lack of belief in the world to come: "As for the dead being raised, haven't you read in the book of Moshe, in the passage about the bush, how God said to him, 'I am the God of Avraham, the God of Yitz'khak and the God of Ya'akov'? He is God not of the dead, but of the living!" (Mark 12:26-27, CJB). The parable of the talents, while it does not specifically mention resurrection or the world to come, is immediately followed by the explicitly second-coming vision of the sheep and the goats, and clearly points to the resurrection as it has the master telling the good servants, "Excellent! You are a good and trustworthy servant. You have been faithful with a small amount, so I will put you in charge of a large amount. Come and join in your master's happiness!" (Matthew 25:21, CJB).

Those of a cynical or non-believing persuasion will say that ideas of an existence after death, an eternal soul, is just human vanity; because man is sentient and more intelligent that animals - who also die - he thinks that he should live for ever; that it offends man's sense of 'being' that he too should simply cease at death. They suggest that man, from the earliest times, has surrounded himself with the imagined worlds of eternity in order to comfort him and provide a psychological cushion against the mortality of his own ego. Others of a less uncharitable outlook, while continuing to deny any resurrection of life after death, will talk about man living on in the memory of successive generations; that man struggles to build a reputation and a lifestyle so that his children and grandchildren may remember him when he is gone, quote his sayings, read his books, and so somehow generate the illusion of life after death in the minds of family, friends and acquaintances. In all but the most exceptional - or infamous - cases, of course, this lasts only for two or three generations at most and is limited to specific families.

The Bible completely rejects these humanistic ideas; its pages are full of the positive expectation that there is a God, that man has an eternal soul, that God will hold each person accountable for their actions in this life, that there are consequences to the choices and decisions we make and that God desires to be involved with our lives and His creation. Rav Sha'ul writes, "If it is only for this life that we have put our hope in Messiah, we are more pitiable than anyone" (1 Corinthians 15:19, CJB). Every person knows deep down inside them that God will judge them for their life here on this earth; the humanistic arguments are simply an excuse to avoid dealing with God and pretend that He doesn't exist, a way of quelling their fears. "But the fact is that Messiah has been raised from the dead, the firstfruits of those who have died" (v. 20, CJB). Our sense of eternity is real, an in-built witness of the truth, so that our text about the death of Aharon is simply confirmation of what we already knew: death is but one of the steps in our eternal path. How important, then, that we should be gathered to our people - the people of God - and not cut off. Yeshua said, **"Yes, this is the will of My Father: that all who see the Son and trust in Him should have eternal life, and that I should raise them up on the Last Day"** (John 6:40, CJB). This is no false promise; this is our life!

Further Study: Romans 4:16-17; Hebrews 11:13-16

Application: Many people find the subject of what happens after death very disturbing and uncomfortable to talk about, but these concerns can be easily set at rest by knowing Yeshua. Could you help someone reach peace in this way this week?

חֻקַּת / בָּלָק׳ו

Hukkat - Statute / Balak - Balak - 6

B'Midbar / Numbers 22:39 - 23:26

B'Midbar/Numbers 23:5 And Adonai put a word in the mouth of Bil'am and He said, "... and thus you shall speak."

וַיָּשֶׂם יהוה דָּבָר בְּפִי בִלְעָם וַיֹּאמֶר ... וְכֹה
v'cho ... vayomer Vil'am b'fiy davar Adonai vayasem

תְדַבֵּר:
t'dabeyr

    This text comes just before Balaam delivers the first of three "blessings" on Israel to Balak, the king of Moab. In the previous verses, we have been told that Balak has hired Balaam to come and curse Israel so that they should not be able to threaten Moab, and that *HaShem* has told Balaam very clearly, "Go with the men, but you shall speak only the word which I shall tell you" (B'Midbar 22:35, NASB). Balaam has repeated this to Balak: "Behold, I have come now to you! Am I able to speak anything at all? The word that God puts in my mouth, that I shall speak" (v. 38, NASB). This text is repeated almost word for word before the second "blessing" in 23:16 and the combination generates some comment on the subject of prophecy. Was this complete dictation - Balaam could say only the exact words that *HaShem* provided, akin to a human tape-recorder - or were the words subject to shaping and interpretation by Balaam's own vocabulary or personality?

    Rashi, who comments only on the second instance (in verse 35) and is convinced that Balaam really wants to curse Israel and will need coercion for anything else to happen, draws a picture of a bridle and a hook: "like a person who pricks [the mouth of] an animal to take it wherever he wishes, [God] told him, 'Against your will, you will go back to Balak [and say ...]'". In Rashi's mind, then, Balaam has no choice over the words that he speaks; while not quite absolute dictation, Balaam is not able to change or modify the message in any way. The Ba'al HaTurim confirms this idea by pointing out that the *gematria* of the word בְּפִי is equivalent to both מַלְאָךְ - angel -

and הַזֹּמֶם - the muzzle; from this he deduces that "God placed an angel as a muzzle in his mouth" to make sure that Balaam only spoke God's words. Milgrom too confirms that "the Lord told him the exact words" and cites "I will raise up a prophet from among their countrymen like you, and I will put My words in his mouth, and he shall speak to them all that I command him" (D'varim 18:18, NASB) to adduce that "and so it is with every prophet."

The Ramban seems to suggest some sympathy with the opposite idea, and explains that in his opinion, Balaam did know and understand what he was saying; that is, he participated in the process. The Ramban says that, "He taught him the words so that he should recite them with his mouth, and he should not forget or omit any part of it", but that in the same way as Moshe is told, "Now therefore, write this song for yourselves, and teach it to the sons of Israel; put it on their lips, in order that this song may be a witness for Me against the sons of Israel" (D'varim 31:19, NASB), Moshe must engage with the people and they must participate with him in learning the song, so Balaam had to learn and absorb what *HaShem* had given him to say.

The prophets themselves speak as if they had ownership in their messages, even if the themes came from God. Jeremiah, for example protests, "I have become a laughingstock all day long; everyone mocks me. For each time I speak, I cry aloud; I proclaim violence and destruction, because for me the word of the Lord has resulted in reproach and derision all day long. But if I say, 'I will not remember Him or speak anymore in His name,' then in my heart it becomes like a burning fire shut up in my bones; and I am weary of holding it in, and I cannot endure it" (Jeremiah 20:7-9, NASB). Hosea is himself a living word of prophecy, speaking out of his own anguish and marital stress of the relationship between God and His people. Jonah was sent to the people of Nineveh, but ran away because he feared the embarrassment that he felt would follow his proclamation of God's wrath in that city; his final argument with God about the gourd shows how much his own personality was involved in being a prophet and bringing prophecy. Speaking about the way that God's word moves within him, Job records "For I am full of words; the spirit within me constrains me. Behold, my belly is like unvented wine, like new wineskins it is about to burst. Let me speak that I may get relief; let me open my lips and answer" (Job 32:18-20, NASB), while the Psalmist describes the process of prophecy in three distinct phases: feeling the sense or emotion of God's word, phrasing and choosing words to express it and then finally speaking it out: "My heart was hot within me; while I was musing the fire burned; then I spoke with my tongue" (Psalm 39:3, NASB).

Despite the standard teaching within rabbinic Judaism that prophecy ceased shortly after the return from the Babylonian exile, there was clearly some understanding within Second Temple Judaism of the way prophecy worked. Following Yeshua's Resurrection and the outpouring of the *Ruach*, the disciples were teaching in the Temple each day; after the healing of the lame man at the gateway to the Temple, Peter and John were arrested by the Temple authorities who, unable to deny that a great miracle had occurred, ordered them not to teach any more in the name of Yeshua. "But Kefa and Yochanan answered, 'You must judge whether it is right in the sight of God to listen to you rather than God. As for us, we can't help talking about what we have actually seen and heard'" (Acts 4:19-20, CJB) - effectively: we must follow the direction of the Spirit. After threatening them - at a human level - the *Sanhedrin* were unable to say or do any more since the public miracle could not be denied.

This, then, provides the context for Rav Sha'ul's teaching on prophecy. "Let two or three prophets speak, while the others weigh what is said. And if something is revealed to a prophet who is sitting down, let the first one be silent. For you can all prophesy one by one, with the result that all will learn something and all will be encouraged. Also, the prophets' spirits are under the prophets' control; for God is not a God of unruliness but of shalom" (1 Corinthians 14:29-33, CJB). First, we see that prophecy is not an unknown or unexpected phenomenon; this is not something that died out four hundred years ago, since no-one would know what it was or how it worked. Secondly, that prophecy is to be weighed and considered by other prophets or those in leadership. Thirdly, so that there is order, everyone doesn't shout out their prophecy at once, but takes time to bring it forth, waiting if necessary until the previous person has finished so giving time for composition and consideration. Lastly, Rav Sha'ul makes it clear that the prophet controls the process. In modern terms, not only is the timing of when to bring the prophecy under the control of the people involved - the prophet themselves, the leaders of the congregation and so on - but that the exact wording and manner of delivery is also under the prophet's control. The Spirit works through the prophet's natural voice, pitch and intonation, accent and - often, but not always - vocabulary.

How do we learn from these things for our congregations today? Primarily, of course, we must recognise that God wants to speak to - to encourage, to challenge and sometimes even to rebuke - His people today as in every age. Whilst congregational leaders may differ as to how exactly this is to be done, tested and received, Rav Sha'ul seems clear: "Do not quench the Spirit; do not despise prophetic utterances. But examine everything carefully; hold fast to that which is good; abstain from every form of evil" (1 Thessalonians 5:19-22, NASB). Secondarily, while some variation is clearly to be expected, prophecy is neither something that should be delivered in King James English, nor swamped in theatrical performance that obscures the message and makes the delivery more important than the content. Prophecy is meant to be understood easily and clearly by those present, in a way that is faithful to the revelation of God's heart that inspired it, so that it can be measured on its own merits rather than being rejected (or despised) because of the packaging. Above all, we must speak the words that God gives us without interpreting those words in the light of our own theological or emotional positions. That way, God will place a word in our mouth and thus we shall speak.

Further Study: Jeremiah 1:9-12; Amos 8:1-2

Application: If you have witnessed the gift of prophecy in operation and it has made you feel uncomfortable, try and distinguish between the message and the messenger. We are all clay vessels, but God can nevertheless speak through any of us. We need to listen and expect Him to speak, especially in these last days.

Hukkat - Statute - 7

B'Midbar / Numbers 21:21 - 22:1

B'Midbar/Numbers 21:22 "Let me pass through your land; we will not turn to field or vineyard, we will not drink well water ..."

אֶעְבְּרָה בְאַרְצֶךָ לֹא נִטֶּה בְּשָׂדֶה וּבְכֶרֶם לֹא
lo oov'cherem b'sadeh niteh lo v'ar'tzecha e'b'rah

נִשְׁתֶּה מֵי בְאֵר
v'eyr mey nishteh

    These were the words of an emissary of peace that Moshe sent to Sichon, the king of the Amorites, when the people of Israel were approaching the Promised Land and wanted to pass peacefully through the land of the Amorites, east of the Dead Sea. Rashi comments that although the Israelites had not been commanded to make peace with them - based on *HaShem* saying to Moshe, "Look! I have given Sichon the Amorite, king of Heshbon, and his land into your hand; begin to take possession and contend with him in battle" (D'varim 2:24, NASB) - they nevertheless sought peace from them. The Ba'al HaTurim adds that since the particle נָא - please - was not included in Moshe's words, as it had been in the case of Edom (see B'Midbar 20:17), Moshe was not really interested in making peace with the Amorites, but sent messengers merely as a gesture. The Midrash Tanchuma (Tanchuma 22) suggests that even though Moshe knew that Sichon would refuse the offer of peace, he still took into consideration *HaShem's* great love of peace and fulfilled the Psalmist's instruction: "Depart from evil, and do good; seek peace, and pursue it" (Psalm 34:14, NASB).

    The Ramban, on the other hand, writes that Moshe was sincerely trying to make peace with Sichon. Moshe knew that the land to the west of the Jordan was "a good land" (D'varim 8:7), the land that was "flowing with milk and honey" (B'Midbar 14:8) and wanted Israel to dwell together there in Israel proper. The whole of Israel was later to tell Reuben, Gad and the half-tribe of Manasseh living east of the Jordan that they must not build an altar there "because the land of your holding is unclean" (Joshua 22:19, JPS); to worship *HaShem* they must "cross over into the land of the Lord's own holding, where the Tabernacle of the Lord abides" (JPS). If Sichon would accept an offer of peace, Moshe reasoned, then Reuven and Gad would not take the land east of the Jordan and Israel would not be split across the river.

Rav Sha'ul, writing to the Messianic community in Rome, tells them, "If possible, so far as it depends on you, be at peace with all men" (Romans 12:18, NASB). That's quite a tough call, bearing in mind what men can be like. Sha'ul is not suggesting that the believers should be like doormats and allow themselves to be walked all over - his emphasis on "so far as it depends on you" means that the believers should make offers of peace when conflict arises, should not offend their neighbours or start arguments, but that they are not responsible when others insist on a fight: be that religiously, legally or physically. We live in an age where everything is apparently tolerated except tolerance and following the God of Israel. Other religions demand - and seem to receive - huge special interest and minority concessions, while the adherents of Judaism and Christianity routinely have their rights and interests ignored or abused. While squeezing extremely risky and security-weakening confidence-building gestures from the state of Israel, world governments play into the hand of extremists, strengthening and hardening their demands beyond the point where any meaningful peace can be made. "From the prophet even to the priest everyone practises deceit. And they heal the brokenness of the daughter of My people superficially, saying, 'Peace, peace,' but there is no peace" (Jeremiah 8:10-11, NASB).

Many quote Yeshua's words when He taught, "Blessed are the peacemakers, for they shall be called sons of God" (Matthew 5:9, NASB), without understanding what making peace really means. Peace making is not at all the same as peace keeping. Keeping the peace seems to consist either of finding some minimum amount of common ground upon which two antagonists can agree, while ignoring the larger and more emotive issues in the hope that the parties will eventually be able to talk about them later once they have come to have some trust in each others' intentions; alternatively, peace keeping consists of appeasing the more aggressive bully-type by giving them more and more of what they want, at the expense of the weaker party, the while assuring everyone - and particularly the one who has actually been forced into giving up something they held dear - that this will definitely be the last time and trying to find some twisted logic to justify such patently unfair treatment. Peace making, on the other hand is a full engagement with the needs of both parties, negotiating a middle-ground settlement that both sides can fully support; peace makers will rebuke both sides equally for their intransigence or failure to keep previous agreements, will not be or pretend to be blind to the hidden or aggressive aspirations of either party, but will have the authority to hammer out a meaningful solution to a conflict. Peace keeping rarely, if ever, produces peace; it is usually based upon a false, delusional or deceptive reading of the situation and as such is hated by God: "My hand will be against the prophets who see false visions and utter lying divinations. They will have no place in the council of My people, nor will they be written down in the register of the house of Israel, nor will they enter the land of Israel, that you may know that I am the Lord God. It is definitely because they have misled My people by saying, 'Peace!' when there is no peace" (Ezekiel 13:9-10, NASB). By contrast, peace making is a long and costly business, often taking significant investment on the part of the peace maker, who must be completely impartial and employ the utmost integrity and even-handedness.

The writer to the Hebrews adds a further dimension: "Keep pursuing shalom with everyone and the holiness without which no one will see the Lord" (Hebrews 12:14, CJB). As well as pursuing peace, it is necessary to pursue holiness at the same time and in equal measure. Holiness means being spiritually whole or sound; of unimpaired innocence and virtue; free from sinful affections; pure in heart; godly; pious; irreproachable; guiltless; acceptable to God. As God is the author of peace and true peace can only be found in Him, peace making must seek to reach an agreement which is acceptable to God, which matches His expressed desires and observes His rules and standards. Peace making must reach a true solution where the parties can embrace each other and seek each other's good, rather than an armed truce - until the next time - enacted by a sulky handshake that is nothing but a thin veneer over an entrenched intention not to perform.

How then should we behave? Few of us are involved with international negotiations or even national matters, except as horrified bystanders looking on and praying for a better outcome than we fear may be the case. On the other hand, all of us are called to be part of God's peace-making corps, reaching out to the world to announce His initiative to make peace with mankind. This call comes "from God, who through the Messiah has reconciled us to Himself and has given us the work of that reconciliation" (2 Corinthians 5:18, CJB). Just as we have been made right with God when we heard the message of salvation in Messiah Yeshua and trusted our lives to Him, so now we are enlisted in heaven's army to help others to find reconciliation - peace with God - in their lives. "Therefore we are ambassadors of the Messiah; in effect, God is making His appeal through us. What we do is appeal on behalf of the Messiah, 'Be reconciled to God!'" (v. 20, CJB)

As God's peace-makers, we are to invest our time and prayers into the lives of others, sharing our lives with them, so that they may see and desire the peace that we have. He has already made the ultimate gesture of reconciliation, giving His son Yeshua to die on the cross for our sins - this is what makes peace possible - but the agreement still needs to be hammered out, received and truly accepted. God is not interested in limp handshakes, guilty and furtive looks and a press release to one's own people in one's own language that denies the substance of the agreement; God is looking for wholehearted and joyful acceptance of His offer of full and complete reconciliation, the start of a frank and open relationship that will last not just a few months, or even years, but a whole lifetime and beyond into eternity. Unlike Moshe, who may or may not have intended to make peace, for a variety of motives, God has clearly declared His hand, has laid His cards on the table and invites everyone to make peace with Him. Our part is to communicate that clearly and unambiguously to everyone that God brings into our path, taking risks, time and trouble as necessary to be peace-makers, not just peace-keepers.

Further Study: Romans 14:17-19; 2 Corinthians 13:11

Application: How do you respond when you are met with a hostile reception to your faith and the message of the gospel? Do you try to invest into that opportunity, to make peace with that person, or do you back away and apologise, trying to keep the peace by keeping quiet? Why not pray that God will give you opportunities to work up your strength and determination to be a kingdom peace-maker.

B'Midbar - Numbers

Balak - Balak

B'Midbar / Numbers 22:2 - 25:9

This portion is sometimes read with the preceding portion - *Hukkat* - so some of the following portions are missing.

רִאשׁוֹן	Aliyah One	B'Midbar/Numbers 22:2 - 12
שֵׁנִי	Aliyah Two	B'Midbar/Numbers 22:13 - 20
רְבִיעִי	Aliyah Four	B'Midbar/Numbers 22:39 - 23:12
חֲמִשִׁי	Aliyah Five	B'Midbar/Numbers 23:13 - 26
שְׁבִיעִי	Aliyah Seven	B'Midbar/Numbers 24:14 - 25:9

Balak - Balak - 1

B'Midbar / Numbers 22:2 - 12

B'Midbar/Numbers 22:2 Now Balak the son of Tzippor saw all that Isra'el had done to the Emori.

וַיַּרְא בָּלָק בֶּן־צִפּוֹר אֵת כָּל־אֲשֶׁר־עָשָׂה
asah   asher kol   eyt   Tzippor ben   Balak   vayar

יִשְׂרָאֵל לָאֱמֹרִי׃
la'Emori   Yisra'el

Balak saw ... and all the people of Moab were afraid! Balak was the king of Moab, one of the kingdoms past which our people would travel on their way to the Land. His spies and intelligence staff brought him all the reports of the battles that Israel had fought and won: the king of Arad (21:1-3); Sichon, king of the Emori (vv. 21-32); Og, king of Bashan (vv. 33-35). Now this people, who had just destroyed the two regional superpowers, were camped on the plains of Moab, opposite Jericho. Balak knew all about it; he had all the details; he saw all that Israel had done - he was afraid, and all his people were afraid. Was Moab next?

So it is with us today. Rav Sha'ul wrote, "our struggle is not against flesh and blood, but against the rulers, against the powers, against the world forces of this darkness, against the spiritual forces of wickedness in the heavenly places" (Ephesians 6:12, NASB). We have an enemy, "the Adversary, [who] stalks about like a roaring lion looking for someone to devour" (1 Peter 5:8, CJB), who sees every move we make and hears every word that comes out of our mouths. His spies and intelligence staff bring him reports of everywhere we go and everything we do. Every time we say the *Sh'ma* and proclaim God's kingdom the demons tremble with fear (James 2:19). It is as if we had flashing blue lights on our heads - in the spiritual realms - Yeshua said, "You are the light for the world. A town built on a hill cannot be hidden" (Matthew 5:14, CJB). But the Scriptures give us the promise: "Resist the devil and he will flee from you" (James 4:7, NASB).

However, more are watching us than the powers of darkness. The writer to the Hebrews tells that "we are surrounded by such a great cloud of witnesses" (Hebrews 12:1, CJB), both those who have gone before and those around us every day. The world also sees everything we do, every unguarded moment, and judges both us and the Kingdom of God by what they see. Whilst we should not be paranoid, we must always endeavour to remember that we are the visible hands and feet of Yeshua in the world today. What would He want us to be displaying to those around us on His behalf?

Surely, we must show that we are not afraid of the giants in the land, that in God's power we can overcome the various trials and temptations that come our way. But more than that, we also have to show that God is merciful and loving, "patient ... not wishing for any to perish but for all to come to repentance" (2 Peter 3:9, NASB).

Further Study: Hebrews 12:1-3; 1 Peter 5:6-9

Application: Stop and pause for a moment today to consider the picture of God and His kingdom that you portray to those around you. Ask God to give you more of the qualities that He wants to reveal in and through your life.

Balak - Balak - 2

B'Midbar / Numbers 22:13 - 20

B'Midbar/Numbers 22:13 And Balaam arose in the morning and he said to the princes of Balak ...

וַיָּקָם בִּלְעָם בַּבֹּקֶר וַיֹּאמֶר אֶל־שָׂרֵי בָלָק
Valak   sarey   el   vayomer baboker   Bil'am   vayakam

This verse comes almost at the end of the first visit of Balak's representatives to Balaam to ask him to come to Moab and curse the people of Israel so that the king of Moab might defeat them and drive them out of his land. Unlike a similar phrase, "And Avraham arose early in the morning" from B'resheet 22:3, which uses the verb שָׁכַם, to get up early, and is usually for the purpose of making an early start on a journey (cf. Joshua 8:14, Hosea 6:4), the active verb here is קוּם, meaning arise or stand. Because of this, the Ramban comments that Balaam was very haughty with these messengers from Balak, implying that they were not worthy enough for him to go with them; the verb קוּם, according to Brown-Driver-Briggs, also being used to convey a hostile or sudden action, becoming powerful, appearing or becoming, as a preliminary to formal speech, or as a superior among inferiors. Balaam's intent, according to Hirsch, was to imply that if higher ranking messengers were sent, with a suitable inducement, then he would come - although in fact it was *HaShem* who had specifically told Balaam not to go with them or cu rse Israel (v. 12).

Yeshua taught about the way we speak when He said, "Let your 'Yes' be a simple 'Yes', and your 'No' a simple 'No'" (Matthew 5:37, CJB). We should say what we mean and mean what we say, without implying or inferring more than our words convey, either in tone or body language. We should strive to be simple and straightforward in our speech, "speaking the truth in love" (Ephesians 4:15, NASB), seeking to build up and encourage each other. For, as Yeshua said, "by your own words you will be acquitted and by your own words you will be condemned" (Matthew 12:37, CJB) - and Balaam's words of dishonesty led ultimately to his demise. (cf. B'Midbar

31:8, 16).

Although the Lord clearly did speak through Balaam, the Sages are unanimous in drawing a line between Balaam and the prophets of Israel. They point to the different ways in which God speaks, the mannerisms and language employed, plus the conduct and behaviour of Balaam, to show that although God did speak through Balaam - even generating the blessing said each day when entering the synagogue: "*Mah Tovu* - How goodly are your tents, O Ya'akov" - it was not a happy relationship as Balaam was not honest in speaking of his dependence on the Lord, or later going against God's commands to give advice that led to many in Israel being seduced into idolatry. If we are not honest in our words, then we too will fall into error and will cause others to fall also.

Further Study: 1 Kings 22:11-23; 2 Thessalonians 2:11-12

Application: We are often unaware how much we communicate by our tone or body language as opposed to our words. Sometimes we convey a completely different message from the one that is coming out of our mouth - damaging or impairing the words of life that Yeshua has given us to say. Why not work on being consistent in your communication today?

Balak - Balak - 4

B'Midbar / Numbers 22:39-23:12

B'Midbar/Numbers 22:39 Balaam went with Balak and they entered Kiryat Hutzot.

וַיֵּלֶךְ בִּלְעָם עִם־בָּלָק וַיָּבֹאוּ קִרְיַת חֻצוֹת:
khootzot kir'yat vayavo'u Balak im Bil'am vayeylech

Our text finds us part-way through the story of Balaam, the gentile sorcerer or prophet (depending on your point of view), who was summoned by Balak the king of Moab to curse the people of Israel as they sat just outside his country. At the beginning of the story we read that "Moab was in great fear because of the people, for they were numerous; and Moab was in dread of the sons of Israel" (22:3, NASB); Moab and Balak, its king, are afraid of the Israelites. As the plot unfolds, "the elders of Moab and the elders of Midian departed with the fees for divination in their hand; and they came to Balaam" (v. 7, NASB), to summon Balaam to curse the threat on Moab's borders. *HaShem* doesn't initially allow Balaam to go, so "Balak again sent leaders, more numerous and more distinguished than the former" (v. 15, NASB) and this time Balaam is permitted to go with them. When they arrive, they are greeted by Balak in person, who rebukes Balaam for the delay: "Did I not urgently send to you to call you? Why did you not come to me?" (v. 37, NASB). The urgency and pitch of the summons and the conversation show us that Balak is really feeling the pressure of having Israel encamped on the border having seen and heard what had happened to Sihon, the king of the Amalekites, and Og, king of Bashan!

Why did Balak take Baalam to Kiryat Hutzot? Rashi translates the name קִרְיַת חֻצוֹת as "a city full of marketplaces" and comments that there were "many men, women and children in its plazas," as if to invoke pity: "have mercy on these people, so that they should not be uprooted." Hirsch suggests that Balak showed him "streets, markets, busy traffic of commerce and full of people ... so that [Balaam] should realise the importance of the mass of innocent inhabitants for whose continued existence he was concerned." By emphasising the number of people whose lives and livelihoods were at risk, it is as if Balak is trying to convince Balaam that, as a conscientious and compassionate king, he has no choice but to get the latter to curse the potential invaders in order to protect his people. Alternatively, we can see Balak using the people as an excuse for wanting to curse Israel - you see what I must do, it is not for myself but for all these - when he wanted to do it himself to protect his kingdom, life, prestige and influence in the region.

The first king of Israel - Saul - fell into the same situation. Sent by *HaShem* to destroy the Amalekites, with specific instructions not to spare people or animals, he and the people did not kill the Amalekite king and kept the best of the sheep and cattle. When challenged about the "bleating of sheep and the lowing of the oxen" (1 Samuel 15:14, NASB) by Samuel, Saul turns round and uses the people as his excuse: "I did obey the voice of the Lord ... but the people took some of the spoil, sheep and oxen ... to sacrifice to the Lord your God at Gilgal" (vv. 20-21, NASB). Saul used the people - as if even as king he could not control them - as the excuse for his own disobedience. Consequently, Saul has the kingdom taken away from him; partly because of his disobedience to God's explicit instructions, but significantly because he was not honest and tried to blame other people for his own sin. Although King David committed both adultery and murder, he was still known as a man after God's heart because when confronted by his sin he confessed it and repented. David's son Solomon wrote, "He who conceals his sins will not succeed; he who confesses and abandons them will gain mercy" (Proverbs 28:13, CJB). We must be honest with God: we do sin and we must confess it to Him so that He can forgive us: "If we claim not to have sin, we are deceiving ourselves, and the truth is not in us" (1 John 1:8, CJB).

Balak used his people as an excuse for hiring Balaam to curse Israel so that he might remain king of Moab and retain his credibility and influence in the region; Saul blamed the people for his weakness and failure to carry out God's commands. Let us not fall into the same trap and try to avoid responsibility for our own shortcomings but instead own up and seek God's forgiveness.

Further Study: Shemot 32:21-24; 2 Samuel 12:7-14; Luke 15:21-24

Application: Do you find yourself pointing the finger at others when things go wrong: "She gave me the apple and I ate" (B'resheet 3:12), or do you come clean before the Lord when you have done or been involved in something that you know does not please God? Now would a good time to recognise and stand up to your own responsibility, so that God can forgive you!

Balak - Balak - 5

B'Midbar / Numbers 23:13 - 26

B'Midbar/Numbers 23:13 "Go, I pray, with me to another place from whence you will see them ..."

לְךְ־נָא אִתִּי אֶל־מָקוֹם אַחֵר אֲשֶׁר תִּרְאֶנּוּ
tir'enu   asher   akheyr   makom   el   itiy   na l'cha

מִשָּׁם
misham

    Balaam having been unable at his first attempt to curse Israel as requested, Balak tries taking him to another vantage point to see if he can do any better. There once again a set of of altars will be built and sacrifices offered in the hope that this will "bribe" God into letting Balaam speak the wanted curse. Rashi tells us that the place was שְׂדֵה צֹפִים, the field of lookouts or watchers, "It was a high place - where the lookout would stand to keep watch, to see if an army would come against the city." Milgrom offers an alternative explanation - that it was a lookout post for "astrological observation or for observing the flight of birds," commonly taken as a sign or omen from the gods. He continues that "the Phoenicians called the astrologer by the same root - צֹפֵי שָׁמַיִם, watcher of the skies."

    This is the second of three attempts to curse Israel that *HaShem* turns around for blessing. Balak provides three different venues: the high places of Ba'al (22:41), the field of watchers/seers (23:14) and רֹאשׁ הַפְּעוֹר - the head of Pe'or - a ritual site of a cult that deified the most basic bodily functions. It is as if, Hirsch suggests, Israel is being attacked at three successive levels to see if there is any weakness to be found. Ba'al - the most popular Canaanite god - was considered the god of Nature and so the source of physical prosperity and material well-being; did Israel have vulnerability to the forces of nature, material growth and decay, prosperity and poverty? Balaam's first answer is that Israel is "a people who dwells apart, and shall not be reckoned among the nations" (v. 9, NASB); Israel's existence is not dependent on the physical world in the same way as the other nations - our continued existence after all the vicissitudes and exigencies of nearly 1900 years of exile out of our own country are a testimony to God preserving the Jewish people regardless of place, circumstance or physical well-being.

The second site focused on the supernatural as if to see whether Israel had a dependency on seers, clairvoyants and astrologers - could they be attacked by magic? Balaam's second answer, then, first rebukes Balak for his assumption that God is fickle or can be manipulated by a few offerings, "God is not a man, that He should lie; nor a son of man, that He should repent; has He said, and will He not do it?" (v. 19, NASB), then continues that "there is no omen against Jacob, nor is there any divination against Israel; at the proper time it shall be said to Jacob and to Israel, what God has done" (v. 23, NASB); in spite of the bad times that were to come in the years when they did pursue the local gods, Israel is fundamentally proof against all supernatural influence and attack because, "the Lord his God is with him, and the shout of a king is among them" (v. 21, NASB) and they will hear God telling them what to do when they need to do it.

Finally, Balak challenges Israel about their inner purity and morals: are Israel's heart and standards pure or do they have an inner addiction or sickness that would make them flawed and eventually rot from the inside out? Balaam's third answer demolishes the question by extolling Israel's dwelling and way of life: "How fair are your tents, O Jacob; your dwellings, O Israel! Like valleys that stretch out, like gardens beside the river ... water shall flow from his buckets" (24:5-7, NASB). Whether the tents during the wanderings of Jacob, or in the houses and mansions of Israel, generation after generation will seek God, will teach His word and His ways to the next generation for the Children of Israel are God's chosen people and they will breed true, passing on a spiritual inheritance that will resist even the basest of depredations.

In the gospels we read of a very similar three-fold process. Immediately after his immersion by John in the Jordan river, Yeshua is led by the *Ruach HaKodesh* into the wilderness for forty days. There He is tempted by the enemy to see if He is vulnerable to the same three challenges to which Israel was subjected. The first venue is the wilderness itself where, after many days of fasting, Yeshua is tempted at a physical level: will He bow to the material needs of His body; the second venue is "the holy city ... the pinnacle of the temple" (Matthew 4:5, NASB) and the challenge is supernatural: will He force a high-profile miracle to jump-start His ministry rather than just waiting for the due process that God has already laid out to work through; the third venue is "a very high mountain" overlooking "all the kingdoms of the world and their glory" (v. 8, NASB) when His basic integrity and inner strength are tested: will He take the short and quick fix to rescue the world but sacrifice His inner self by worshipping the devil? In all three cases, just as with Israel, the answer comes directly from God's word; in Israel's case, a prophetic word spoken through Balaam, in Yeshua's case, the written words of the *Torah*, God's revealed word through Moshe at Sinai.

The gospels also record another three-fold test, that of Simon Peter, the bluff and forthright fisherman and one of Yeshua's inner circle of disciples. In three connected but separate venues - "outside in the courtyard" (Matthew 26:69, NASB), "out [by] the gateway" (v. 71, NASB) and later, "after about an hour had passed" (Luke 22:59, NASB) - Peter denied knowing Yeshua, being one of His disciples and even being with Yeshua when He was arrested. Almost all commentators connect this three-fold denial with the tripartite restoration process in John 21:15-17.

If Yeshua, Israel and Peter were tempted or tested in this way, examined to see if they had flaws or weaknesses that would allow the enemy to curse them, to destroy their ministries or cause them to deny their faith and calling, how much more so should we expect to be challenged in the same way. The onslaught of the media, peer pressure from friends, acquaintances and work colleagues, sometimes even physical interventions such as car accidents, sickness and bank managers, all conspire to destroy our integrity, defeat our walk with the Lord, or walk away from our identities or calling as God's people. In every case, God provides the resources for us to survive: "with the temptation [God] will also provide the way out, so that you will be able to endure" (1 Corinthians 10:13, CJB), "so that when the evil day comes, you will be able to resist; and when the battle is won, you will still be standing" (Ephesians 6:13, CJB).

Further Study: 2 Corinthians 11:1-4; Ephesians 6:10-18

Application: If you are going through trials and temptations at this time, take comfort that you are not the only one and that not only is God continuing to work His purposes out in your life, but that the discomfort is a part of the discipling process (cf. Hebrews 12:7-11) that is making you more like Yeshua and better able to comfort and encourage others.

Balak - Balak - 7

B'Midbar / Numbers 24:14-25:9

B'Midbar/Numbers 24:14 Come, I will disclose to you what this people will do to your people in the Last Days.

לְכָה אִיעָצְךָ אֲשֶׁר יַעֲשֶׂה הָעָם הַזֶּה לְעַמְּךָ
l'amcha hazeh ha'am ya'aseh asher iy'atz'cha l'cha

בְּאַחֲרִית הַיָּמִים:
hayamiym b'akhariyt

These words introduce Balaam's fourth and final pronouncement concerning Israel to Balak, the king of Moab. During each of the preceding speeches, Balaam's focus has been moving away in time and now he sees far ahead to the Last Days, the אַחֲרִית הַיָּמִים. Nachmanides describes the sequence: in 23:7-10, Balaam first says that Israel is now the people that dwell apart, "For the Lord's portion is His people; Jacob is the allotment of His inheritance" (D'varim 32:9, NASB); in the second oracle 23:18-24, Balaam adds that *HaShem* is with them and that they will conquer the Land and kill its inhabitants; in the third prophecy 24:3-9, Balaam sees Israel dwelling and multiplying in the Land, appointing a king who will defeat Agag, and David's kingdom being exalted, "David realized that the Lord had established him as king over Israel, and that his kingdom was highly exalted, for the sake of His people Israel" (1 Chronicles 14:2, NASB). Now, in the fourth and longest declaration 24:14-25, Balaam uses the phrases "in the Last Days" (v. 14) and "I see him, but not now; I behold him, but not near" (v. 17, NASB) to show that he is glimpsing far beyond the centuries of history to the times of Messiah. The *Sforno* proposes that Balaam is telling Balak that "the evil that this people will do to your people will not happen in your day, and you will have nothing to fear" and connects it with a wider prophecy about the Messianic age when Judah and Ephraim "will swoop down on the slopes of the Philistines on the west; together they will plunder the sons of the east; they will possess Edom and Moab; and the sons of Ammon will be subject to them" (Isaiah 11:14, NASB).

The word אִיעָצְךָ - a 1cs *Qal* prefix form, "I will", from the root יָעַץ, with a 2ms object suffix, "you", could have several meanings. Davidson suggests "to counsel, advise; to take counsel, decree; to direct or to instruct". The Sforno claims that this refers to the advice Balaam gave Balak later, off camera, to cause Israel's downfall by sexual temptation. Nachmanides, while agreeing that the normal meaning would be "I counsel you", prefers "I will tell you the purpose", aligning it to the verse "This is the purpose (הָעֵצָה) that is purposed (הַיְּעוּצָה) concerning the whole earth" (Isaiah 14:26, ESV) and "Therefore hear the purpose of the Lord (עֲצַת־יהוה) that He has purposed (יָעַץ) against Edom" (Jeremiah 49:20). *Targum Onkelos*, wanting to make sure that both aspects are covered, translates the one verb as if were two: "I will advise you what you should do and I will point out to you ...".

What is it that Balaam, a Gentile prophet or some would say sorcerer, can see in his vision? His words "a star shall come out of Jacob, and a sceptre shall rise out of Israel" (v. 17, ESV) have long been considered part of the Bible's messianic prophecies: that a mighty ruler should arise from the Jewish nation. Rabbi Akiva changed just one letter in Shimon bar Kochba's name (כוסבא to כוכבא) to name him "Son of the Star" and give him messianic status during the second Jewish revolt in 132-135CE; the rabbis later named him "Son of Disappointment" (כוזיבא) and the significance of the prophecy has been played down in Jewish expectations since. The sceptre had previously been mentioned by Ya'akov's final blessings to his sons: "The sceptre shall not depart from Judah, nor the ruler's staff from between his feet, until tribute comes to him; and to him shall be the obedience of the peoples" (B'resheet 49:10, ESV).

The star motif re-appears in the birth narratives of Yeshua. The magi who have come from the east ask, "Where is He who has been born King of the Jews? For we saw His star in the east, and have come to worship Him" (Matthew 2:2, NASB). Ancient peoples would "read" the stars in order to determine the occurrence of events and Balaam's prophecy had spread far from its original saying in the land of Moab, so that the whole world would have known that the Jewish people were expecting a king figure to rise from among them who would rout their enemies and restore the Davidic dynasty. In Roman times, messianic expectation was acute and we know that there were several messianic "pretenders" who claimed to be the Messiah around the time when Yeshua was born.

Yeshua Himself claims the title in the book of Revelation: "I, Yeshua, have sent My angel to give you this testimony for the Messianic communities. I am the Root and Offspring of David, the bright Morning Star" (Revelation 22:16, CJB) and it is applied to Him by Peter, both confirming Him as the object of prophecy and looking to His return: "We have the prophetic word made more sure, to which you do well to pay attention as to a lamp shining in a dark place, until the day dawns and the morning star arises in your hearts" (2 Peter 1:19, NASB).

We, then, are placed in a similar position as Balaam. While our knowledge does not come from divination or occult practices, we can nevertheless see the days of Messiah. Those days must be at least 3,500 years sooner now than they were then, so the Sforno's suggestion that Balaam meant "it won't happen in your day" is no longer valid for us; in fact, many followers of the God of Israel - be they Christians, Messianic, Orthodox or Chassidic Jews - live in a high state of excitement. We see biblical prophecy being fulfilled before our eyes and are eagerly awaiting Messiah's arrival. We too have the privilege of being able to say, "Come, and let me tell you about the Last Days", but we have the hope that Yeshua will return in our lifetimes.

How thrilling to be able to share the Gospel with those same words: "a star shall arise in Jacob; the sceptre shall come from Israel", and know that we are talking about the Yeshua that we know in our hearts as the risen Lord and Messiah. When He returns to Jerusalem, "in that day His feet will stand on the Mount of Olives, which is in front of Jerusalem on the east; and the Mount of Olives will be split in its middle" (Zechariah 14:4, NASB). He will subdue all the nations under His authority "and His rule shall extend from sea to sea and from ocean to land's end" (9:10, JPS). God's judgements and standards will apply throughout the whole earth "for out of Tziyon will go forth Torah, the word of Adonai from Yerushalayim" (Micah 4:2, CJB). This is good news indeed and not only do we have it, but we also have an obligation to share it with all who will hear, that the days might be shortened and His return hastened in the earth.

Further Study: Hosea 3:4-5; 2 Timothy 3:1; Revelation 11:15-17

Application: How could you present the good news about the imminent return of the Lord to someone who needs to hear? A good place to start is by asking Him to share His urgency with you so that, like Balaam, you find yourself speaking out God's word in the most unlikely places!

Pinkhas - Pinchas

B'Midbar / Numbers 25:10 - 30:1

רִאשׁוֹן	Aliyah One	B'Midbar/Numbers 25:10 - 26:4
שֵׁנִי	Aliyah Two	B'Midbar/Numbers 26:5 - 51
שְׁלִישִׁי	Aliyah Three	B'Midbar/Numbers 26:52 - 27:5
רְבִיעִי	Aliyah Four	B'Midbar/Numbers 27:6 - 23
חֲמִשִׁי	Aliyah Five	B'Midbar/Numbers 28:1 - 15
שִׁשִׁי	Aliyah Six	B'Midbar/Numbers 28:16 - 29:11
שְׁבִיעִי	Aliyah Seven	B'Midbar/Numbers 29:12 - 30:1

פִּינְחָס א'

Pinkhas - Pinchas - 1

B'Midbar / Numbers 25:10 - 26:4

B'Midbar/Numbers 25:11 ... so I did not consume the Children of Israel in My zeal

וְלֹא־כִלִּיתִי אֶת־בְּנֵי־יִשְׂרָאֵל בְּקִנְאָתִי
b'kin'atiy   Yisra'el   b'ney   et   chilitiy   v'lo

    The last word in our reading is variously translated zeal (as here and the NIV), jealousy (NASB) and even vengeance (Stones). Pinchas has just abrogated all the *Torah's* careful instructions about fair trials, the need for warning and witness, and in his zeal for God and His righteousness has killed a man, a prince from the tribe of Simeon. The Sages in the *Jerusalem Talmud* state that Moshe and the Elders did not approve of Pinchas' actions and were about to rebuke him when God intervened by speaking these words - thus showing that Pinchas had acted in line with God's own zeal. God's anger and jealousy had been aroused by the Israelites committing harlotry with the Moabites and worshipping their idols.

    In Zechariah 8:2 the prophet uses the words from the same root three times in a single verse to describe the intensity of emotion that the Lord feels over Zion, the city of Jerusalem: "I am zealous for Tziyon, zeal, great and burning, I am zealous for her." Remember also the way that Yeshua said, "Yerushalayim, Yerushalayim! You kill the prophets! You stone those who are sent to you! How often I wanted to gather your children, just as a hen gathers her chickens under her wings, but you refused" (Matthew 23:37, CJB).

    Clearly, there are some things that God is passionate about, and the Scriptures tell us that these are things He expects us to be passionate about as well. Rav Sha'ul tells us "[Yeshua the Messiah] gave Himself for us, that He might redeem us from every lawless deed and purify for Himself a people for His own possession, zealous for good deeds" (Titus 2:14, NASB). Yeshua is zealous that we should be a holy people, totally set apart and committed exclusively to Him, and He is looking for us to be zealous about doing good deeds which, Rav Sha'ul tells us, is why we were created. "For we are His workmanship, created in Messiah Yeshua for good works, which God prepared beforehand that we should walk in them" (Ephesians 2:10, NASB). We must only be careful that we are zealous for God's works and not our own.

Further Study: Titus 3:9; 1 Peter 3:13

Application: Have you fallen away from from zeal and passion for the things of God, for His people and for the good works that He has called us to? How could you get back on target today?

פִּינְחָס ב'

Pinkhas - Pinchas - 2

B'Midbar / Numbers 26:5 - 51

B'Midbar/Numbers 26:5 [to] Hanoch, the Hanochite family, to Pallu, the Palluite family

חֲנוֹךְ מִשְׁפַּחַת הַחֲנֹכִי לְפַלּוּא מִשְׁפַּחַת
Khanoch mish'pakhat hakhanochiy l'Falu mish'pakhat

הַפַּלֻּאִי׃
hapaloo'iy

    In this naming and counting of the people of Israel, which goes through to verse 51 for the tribes other than Levi, and continues to the end of the chapter with the Levite families, the Rabbis note and comment upon the apparent redundancy of the formula, "to Fred, the Freditc family" (Maskil LeDavid). Rashi provides a two-fold explanation. Firstly, he points out, the mechanism for turning 'Fred' into 'Fredite' is adding a ה to the front of the name and a י to the end of the name - both letters that are found in the tetragrammaton - the four-letter ineffable name of God in the Hebrew Scriptures. Secondly, he mentions that in attempts to humiliate the Israelites the nations would say that it was pointless to have elaborate genealogical records of tribal descent since it must be presumed that the Egyptians must have had their way with the Israelite women just as the men were forced slaves in the mud-pits. Putting the two together, Rashi suggests that this textual device is God's way of saying that the family called after Hanoch really is Hanoch's natural family, that Pallu's family is composed of Pallu's own natural sons - that he is their father and so on for all the tribes and families: God protected the purity and descent of our people.

    The Bible talks in very patrilineal terms: that sons should be like their fathers, that sons inherit from their fathers: *cohen*, Levite, tribes and families, family and tribe land allocations. Little wonder that asked by His *talmidim* to show them the Father, Yeshua said, "I and the Father are One" (John 10:30). The setting for Yeshua's famous parable about the prodigal son is an inheritance issue: who will inherit not only the land, the family title and authority, but lifestyle and position in society; who will be like the father in the story. Talking of David's son Solomon, *HaShem* said, "I will be his father and he shall be My son; and I will not take My lovingkindness away from him" (1 Chronicles 17:13, NASB).

It was this very issue of parenthood that brought a very sharp exchange between Yeshua and the *P'rushim* in Jerusalem. In John chapter 8, Yeshua had said that the Father testified on His behalf (v. 18), then "You know neither Me nor My Father; if you knew Me, you would know My Father" (v. 19, CJB). They replied that they were sons of Avraham (v. 39) and Yeshua answered, "You belong to your father, Satan, and want to carry out your father's desires ... Whoever belongs to God listens to what God says; the reason you don't listen is that you don't belong to God" (vv. 44, 47, CJB). People do what their family upbringing has conditioned them towards; people are very like their parents. Yeshua said that knowing the truth and obeying Him would set us free (vv. 31-32): free from generational habits and behaviour, free to serve God.

Further Study: Ephesians 3:14-19; Hosea 6:1-3

Application: Who do we behave like? Do we follow the behaviour patterns of the world, or do we behave like Yeshua, like our Father in heaven? If God has been speaking to you about breaking or changing some habits that you might have had for a long time, now is the time to be free.

פִּינְחָס ג'

Pinkhas - Pinchas - 3

B'Midbar / Numbers 26:52 - 27:5

B'Midbar/Numbers 26:53 To these the land shall be divided, in an inheritance, in the number of names.

לָאֵלֶּה תֵּחָלֵק הָאָרֶץ בְּנַחֲלָה בְּמִסְפַּר שֵׁמוֹת:
la'eyleh teykhaleyk ha'aretz b'nakhalah b'mis'par sheymot

    The Israelites are now in the Plains of Mo'av, by the Jordan river, opposite Jericho (B'Midbar 26:3) and Moshe and Elazar the son of Aharon have just taken a census of the people before preparing to enter the Land. Now *HaShem* gives instructions as to how the Land is to be divided between the tribes. *Rashi* comments that the 'these' in this verse means that the division was to be done according to the census now, and not according to the status or number of families some years later when the Land has been conquered; by then some families may have lost members in combat, while others have grown due to marriage or childbirth. The *Sforno* points out that this way of dividing the Land enabled the fulfillment of Ya'akov's death-bed prophecy to his sons: to Shimon, who was numerically the smallest tribe at the time of entry, was given several pockets of land, rather than one contiguous piece so that Joshua 19:9 records, "Out of the portion of the children of Judah was the inheritance of the children of Simeon" (KJV) so fulfilling, "I will divide them in Ya'akov" (B'resheet 49:7, CJB).

    The physical division of the Land was done both by tribe and by number so that the area and value of the land allocated to each descendant of Ya'akov should be equal. This demonstrates a kingdom principle that Rav Sha'ul writes about: "[in Messiah] there is neither Jew nor Gentile, neither slave nor freeman, neither male nor female; for in union with the Messiah Yeshua you are all one" (Galatians 3:28, CJB). What is Sha'ul saying? Simply that in exactly the same way that the quality and quantity of the land inheritances were balanced to give every Israelite the same value, so believers in Messiah Yeshua - from whatever racial background, gender or social status - all share the same spiritual inheritance in Messiah. No-one is disadvantaged or discriminated against. Given the social order of his day, Sha'ul obviously had to repeat this message several times, for we find him saying it again: "The new self allows no room for discriminating between Gentile and Jew, circumcised and uncircumcised, foreigner, savage, slave, free man; on the contrary, in all, the Messiah is everything" (Colossians 3:11, CJB).

However, just as some Israelites had many acres of poorer quality scrub-land, fine for grazing but no good for intensive horticulture, whilst others had only a few acres of rich land, excellent for vineyards, olive groves or fruit trees, yet others having mid-sized holdings suitable for cereal production, so it is with the roles and identities of believers in the body of Messiah. "For indeed the body is not one part but many. If the foot says, 'I'm not a hand, so I'm not a part of the body,' that doesn't make it stop being part of the body" (1 Corinthians 12:14-15, CJB). We come together with our different gifts, callings and abilities to build up the body and give glory to God.

Further Study: 1 Corinthians 12:12-26; Romans 12:4-8

Application: Be encouraged today with what the Lord has given you to do. Not only has He made you unique, but He has placed you where you can bring your gifts to bear and help others to grow as they share themselves with you. Go to it, for this is the way the body works!

פִּינְחָס ד'

Pinkhas - Pinchas - 4

B'Midbar / Numbers 27:6 - 23

B'Midbar/Numbers 27:7 The daughters of Tzelophehad are right in their words.

כֵּן בְּנוֹת צְלָפְחָד דֹּבְרֹת

dov'rot Tz'laph'khad b'not keyn

Since the literal translation of the verse would be: "Thus the daughters of Tzelophehad are speaking", which is difficult to understand in context, a number of the commentators try to explain what this means. The word דֹּבְרֹת is a feminine plural *Qal* participle of the verb דָּבַר, to speak, which is almost always used in the *Pi'el* stem and hardly ever in *Qal*; it is used only once in the whole of the Tanakh with this spelling. The Ba'al HaTurim points out that a Masoretic note connects it with 1 Kings 5:23 where a different spelling of the word is translated as the noun 'rafts' and suggests that Tzelophehad's daughters were as full of wisdom as the sea is full of water (cf. Isaiah 11:9); the Sages commented that these women were wise, righteous and expositors of the *Torah* (*b. Bava Batra* 119*b*).

Rashi starts by focusing on the word כֵּן, positing that the word should be understood as *Targum Onkelos* renders it: 'properly'; we might say 'correctly' or 'accurately'. Rashi's sense here is that "their eye saw that which the eye of Moshe did not see"; the daughters of Tzelophehad had understood an aspect of the laws on inheritance that Moshe had not yet grasped. Rashi goes on to make another comment: "They claimed correctly - fortunate is the person whose words the Holy One, Blessed is He, confirms" (*Sifre* 134). On most occasions, the initiative is with God: He gives commands, judgements and explanations - Moshe relays these to the people; but here, Tzelophehad's daughters have originated a legal point and God is confirming that they have spoken correctly.

In the gospels, Yeshua talks about two people who built houses - one upon the rock, one upon sand - and the consequences of building on the right - or wrong - foundation. These verses have been used by generations of evangelists to encourage people to make a commitment to Yeshua.

However, consider how those words start: "Therefore everyone who hears these words of Mine and acts upon them ..." (Matthew 7:24, NASB). Whenever the text uses that word 'therefore', we have to consider what has immediately preceded the current verse because 'therefore' introduces a summary or a set of consequences of what has gone before. In this case, the previous verses are among the more disturbing things that Yeshua says: "Many will say to Me on that day, 'Lord, Lord, did we not prophesy in Your name, and in Your name cast out demons, and in Your name perform many miracles?' And then I will declare to them, 'I never knew you; depart from Me, you who practice lawlessness" (vv. 22-23, NASB), and before that Yeshua has been talking about good trees and bad trees and the fruit that they bear, with the instruction, "So then, you will know them by their fruits" (v. 20, NASB). The endurance and collapse of the houses is thus a consequence of the building process - God has confirmed the true state of the person by bringing rain and floods into their lives and the condition and durability of the house becomes obvious to all.

Rav Sha'ul takes up the same theme in his letter to the Philippians: "More than that, I count all things to be loss ... that I may know Him, and the power of His resurrection and the fellowship of His sufferings, being conformed to His death; in order that I may attain to the resurrection from the dead" (Philippians 3:8,10-11, NASB). At first reading, this might appear to be saying that Sha'ul is expecting to earn his resurrection by performing miracles (the power of His resurrection), suffering and giving up his life as a martyr. A closer reading, however, shows that Sha'ul is actually saying the same thing as Yeshua: the miracles, the suffering and the martyrdom are both the rain and floods and the fruit of knowing Yeshua. Sha'ul's house stood, rather than collapsing, in spite of everything that the world threw at him, because it was founded upon Yeshua; the fact that it continued to stand was the living proof - or fruit - of his relationship with God. As Sha'ul said: "I press on in order that I may lay hold of that for which also I was laid hold of by Messiah Yeshua" (v. 12, NASB). Gods purpose, which He would accomplish, was that Sha'ul should stand, so Sha'ul pressed on - co-operated with God's process - to reveal the fruit that God had planned all along.

Further Study: 1 Peter 1:3-5; Acts 5:34-39

Application: Are you blessed by seeing your words and life being confirmed by God or is your life always crumbling around your ears? Take stock today and consider what fruit your life is showing and what that tells you about the state of your relationship with God. He wants us all to bear good fruit.

פִּינְחָס 'ה

Pinkhas - Pinchas - 5

B'Midbar / Numbers 28:1 - 15

B'Midbar/Numbers 28:2 My offerings, My food for My fires, the aroma of My satisfaction, you shall keep watch to offer to Me in its appointed time.

אֶת־קָרְבָּנִי לַחְמִי לְאִשַּׁי רֵיחַ נִיחֹחִי תִּשְׁמְרוּ
tish'm'ru niykhokhiy reyakh l'ishay lakhmiy karbaniy et

לְהַקְרִיב לִי בְּמוֹעֲדוֹ:
b'mo'adi liy l'hak'riyv

The word תִּשְׁמְרוּ - *Qal*, prefix, 2mp from the root שָׁמַר[10], whose meanings range from "guard, protect, watch" to "observe" - is here translated "you shall keep watch" following the general rule that the prefix form denotes incomplete action, often translated in the future tense. Rashi comments: "the *cohanim*, Levites and Israelites should be standing over it. From here they learned and instituted מַעֲמָדוֹת, groups of watchers." Other commentators confirm that because the *Torah* says "you shall keep watch to offer" rather than just "you shall keep offering", the offering must be physically watched while it is prepared and offered; a representative group from all three sections of the Israelite community must be present to ensure that it is done at the right time, that it is done properly, and even that it is done at all. Milgrom points out that is was common to the religions of the surrounding nations that a sacrifice had to be offered at the right time and that the gods would punish people who brought offerings at the wrong time.

The Sages of the *Talmud* collected together (*b.* Ta'anit 27a) the biblical references that showed this understanding being put into practice. The record in 1 Chronicles tells us first that the Israelites, Levites and priests were "enrolled by genealogy in their villages, whom David and Samuel the seer

---

10. Not to be confused with its synonym שָׁמַע, to hear or listen, which is also often taken to have a set of meanings that include "observe" or "obey".

appointed in their office of trust" (9:22, NASB), then that the Levites were organised into watches or shifts: "their position - מַעֲמָדָם, place of standing - is at the side of the sons of Aharon" (23:28) and "to keep watch - וְלִשְׁמֹר - over the Tent of Meeting, the holy place and their kinsmen the sons of Aharon" (v. 32). In the next chapter David established the divisions of the priests: "these were their offices for their ministry when they came in to the house of the Lord according to the ordinance given to them through Aharon their father" (24:15, NASB). Lastly, the people are also included as David set Levites over the tribes on the west and east of the Jordan, "concerning all the labour of Adonai and for the service of the king" (26:32) so that alongside their civil responsibilities, the Israelites would also have their place in the service at the Temple.

We know from the gospel accounts that Yeshua's crucifixion on the stake was a very public affair, just outside the gates of the city of Jerusalem; so designed by the Roman authorities as a deterrent to others who might be tempted to disobey the Roman rule. No-one entering or leaving the city could avoid seeing the sight and the Romans took care to ensure that everyone knew what was going on by having an inscription above Yeshua's head: "Therefore this inscription many of the Jews read, for the place where Yeshua was crucified was near the city; and it was written in Hebrew, Latin and in Greek" (John 19:20, NASB). The crucifixion was witnessed by the crowds: "And when all the crowd that had gathered to watch the spectacle saw the things that had occurred, they returned home beating their breasts" (Luke 23:48, CJB), by the women: "Nearby Yeshua's execution stake stood His mother, His mother's sister Miryam the wife of K'lofar, and Miryam from Magdala" (John 19:25, CJB), the priests: "Likewise the head Cohanim jeered at Him, along with the Torah-teachers and elders" (Matthew 27:41, CJB), and at least one of the disciples: "When Yeshua saw His mother and the talmid whom He loved standing there ..." (John 19:26, CJB). Just as the Temple sacrifices were watched by all those concerned - *Cohanim*, Levites and Israel - so Yeshua's execution was watched by all those affected including, perhaps unwittingly in their case, the Romans as representatives of the Gentiles now to be brought near through this supreme sacrifice. Not only did the Romans serve in the role normally carried out by the priests for animal sacrifices in the Temple, by carrying out His execution, the centurion was also to be a personal witness: "When the Roman officer saw what had happened, he began to praise God and said, 'Surely this man was innocent!'" (Luke 23:47, CJB).

The Scriptures are also at pains to tell us that the timing of Yeshua's death was neither wrong nor by accident. Speaking to the crowds on the morning of *Shavuot*, Peter explained that Yeshua was "delivered up according to the definite plan and foreknowledge of God" (Acts 2:23, ESV). Just a few days later, Peter added, "what God foretold by the mouth of all the prophets, that His Messiah would suffer, He thus fulfilled" (3:18, ESV). Rav Sha'ul is even more explicit: "For while we were still helpless, at the right time, the Messiah died on behalf of ungodly people" (Romans 5:6, CJB). So in every respect, Yeshua's sacrifice was *kosher*: it was in the right place, at the right time and watched by the representatives of all those responsible for and affected by it.

Are we similarly *kosher* in our witness and work for Yeshua and the Kingdom of God? Certainly there are some actions that are to be private affairs - such as prayer and charity - but there is no indication that the twelve and the other first disciples hid their lights under bushels or night-stands! The lame man at the Temple gate was very publicly healed in broad daylight, in front of a large crowd, so that the Temple authorities had to confess: "Why, anyone in Yerushalayim can see that a remarkable miracle has come about through them - we can't possibly deny that" (Acts 4:16, CJB). The text goes on, "With great power the emissaries continued testifying to the resurrection of the Lord Yeshua, and they were all held in high regard" (v. 33, CJB) so that "day after day the Lord kept adding to them those who were being saved" (2:47, CJB). Rav Sha'ul worked in the same way: "A man living in Lystra could not use his feet ... [Sha'ul] said with a loud voice, 'Stand up on your feet!' He jumped up and began to walk. When the crowd saw what Sha'ul had done, they began to shout ... 'The gods have come down to us'" (14:8-11, CJB). Has the time come for our generation of believers to become a lot bolder and more public? Perhaps we need less time hidden away in our buildings and more time in public, proclaiming the Kingdom of God and inviting people to join!

Further Study: Matthew 24:45-46; Galatians 4:4-5

Application: Do you long to see an outpouring of God's power and people flocking to enter the Kingdom of God in your life and congregation? Speak to your pastor or rabbi today to see what you can do and to share your vision with him to push back the forces of darkness and see the Kingdom of God advancing as the Scriptures say.

פִּינְחָס ו׳

Pinkhas - Pinchas - 6

B'Midbar / Numbers 28:16 - 29:11

B'Midbar/Numbers 28:19 ... two bulls, sons of the herd, one ram and seven year-old male lambs ...

פָּרִים בְּנֵי־בָקָר שְׁנַיִם וְאַיִל אֶחָד וְשִׁבְעָה
v'shiva   ekhad   v'ayil   sh'nayim vakar b'ney   pariym

כְּבָשִׂים בְּנֵי שָׁנָה
shana b'ney ch'vasiym

    This set of offerings is the major part - with their grain offerings - of the מוּסָף or additional offering that is made on the first day of the festival of unleavened bread, the fifteenth day of Aviv, the first month of the religious year, now called Nissan. The text tells us, "You shall present these besides the burnt offering of the morning, which is a for continual burnt offering" (B'Midbar 28:23, NASB). These offerings are typical of those prescribed in chapters 28 and 29 of B'Midbar for the festivals in the Jewish calendar from the weekly *shabbat* and monthly new-moon offerings to the three רְגָלִים - pilgrimage festivals - *Pesach*, *Shavuot* and *Sukkot* and the autumn holy days. Although Ezekiel's specification of the offerings in the rebuilt temple are slightly different - "And during the seven days of the feast [the prince, הַנָּשִׂיא] shall provide as a burnt offering to the Lord seven bulls and seven rams without blemish on every day of the seven days, and a male goat daily for a sin offering" (Ezekiel 45:23, NASB) - it is clear that these are significant occasions and particular lists of sacrifices. What is going on?

    Rashi, quoting from R'Moshe HaDarshan, explains that these offerings symbolise the patriarchs: "Bulls: corresponding to Abraham, as it says, 'Then Abraham ran to the cattle' (B'resheet 18:7); rams, corresponding to the ram of Yitzkhak (B'resheet 22:13); lambs, corresponding to Ya'akov, 'Ya'akov segregated the lambs' (B'resheet 30:40)."[11] In this and other

---

11. Other symbolic representations of the patriarchs are known; at least two are tied to the pilgrimage festivals. In one of these schemes, Abraham corresponds to Pesach because he

pictures of the offerings, Rashi and other commentators see a memorial of things, people or events of the past. They have become a way of remembering the past, of bringing to mind what God has done in the past by reviewing and rehearsing the events, of anchoring faith for the present in God's consistency and faithfulness in His earlier actions and miracles. Hirsch comments: "On the fifteenth, the nation links itself together to a חַג - a feast or festival, from a root meaning a circle dance - to a festive circle around God and His Sanctuary, with the *matzot* in our hands for seven days, we acknowledge how it is God and God alone whom we have to thank for the freedom and independence we enjoy, and that we entered the upraising and free-making service of God out of the depressing and down-casting spirit of service of Pharaoh."

When the Israelites crossed over the Jordan river to enter the land of Canaan, the Promised Land that God had sworn to give to our people as our inheritance, Joshua was told to "Take for yourselves twelve men from the people, one man from each tribe, and command them, saying, 'Take up for yourselves twelve stones from here out of the middle of the Jordan, from the place where the priests' feet are standing firm, and carry them over with you, and lay them down in the lodging place where you will lodge tonight'" (Joshua 4:2-3, NASB). Moshe had previously been told to tear down and smash any standing stones and pillars that were found in the Land, because they were memorials to the idols and false gods that the pagan nations worshipped. Joshua now tells the people: "Cross again to the ark of the Lord your God into the middle of the Jordan, and each of you take up a stone on his shoulder, according to the number of the tribes of the sons of Israel. Let this be a sign among you, so that when your children ask later, saying, 'What do these stones mean to you?' then you shall say to them, 'Because the waters of the Jordan were cut off before the ark of the covenant of the Lord; when it crossed the Jordan, the waters of the Jordan were cut off.' So these stones shall become a memorial to the sons of Israel forever" (vv. 5-7, NASB). These twelve stones are to be set up as a permanent reminder of what *HaShem* has done that day, the miracle of the Jordan river parting to let our people cross into the Land. It is significant that when the prophet Elijah faced the prophets of Ba'al on Mt. Carmel, "Elijah took twelve stones according to the number of the tribes of

---

said "Knead and make cakes" (B'resheet 18:6) meaning *Pesach matzot*; Yitzkhak corresponds to *Shavuot*, for the sound of the ram's horn when the *Torah* was given came from the the horn of the ram which was given in his place; Ya'akov corresponds to *Sukkot* for the *Torah* tells as that, "And for his livestock he made shelters (sukkot)" (B'resheet 33:17). An alternative arrangement still has Abraham representing *Pesach* for he excelled in the trait of kindness and the Exodus from Egypt was a unique example of God's kindness; Ya'akov represents *Shavuot* because he is described as "abiding in the tents" (B'resheet 25:27), naturally - according to the Sages - the study tents; Yitzkhak who was consecrated as an offering, then corresponds to *Sukkot* which is the festival on which most offerings are brought (*Be'er BaSadeh*).

the sons of Jacob, to whom the word of the Lord had come, saying, 'Israel shall be your name.' So with the stones he built an altar in the name of the Lord, and he made a trench around the altar, large enough to hold two measures of seed" (1 Kings 18:31-32, NASB), just as the breastplate that the *Cohen Gadol* wore into the presence of God was decorated with stones: "and the stones were corresponding to the names of the sons of Israel; they were twelve, corresponding to their names, engraved with the engravings of a signet, each with its name for the twelve tribes" (Shemot 39:14, NASB). In the latter case, the stones were not in case God should, God forbid, have a senior moment and forget who the Israelites were, but as a token memorial so that not only did the High Priest represent the people before God, but a token of each of the tribes was taken into God's presence with the *Cohen Gadol* every time he wore his ceremonial uniform and went into the Holy of Holies.

Parents and grandparents are blessed today with something that previous generations of 150 or more years ago could not have: being able to take, keep and show many pictures of their children and grandchildren. Go into almost any modern home and you will see proudly displayed frames with pictures of "the first step", "graduation", "first dance" - all milestone events in a child's life, captured and preserved in full colour for posterity. Compare that with the few black-and-white or sepia pictures from 1850 to the 1930s, often formal posed shots, with a significant price attached. Then consider what came before; only drawings and sketches, laboriously done by the hand of an artist, be that professional or amateur. Those of us who can trace their ancestry back to, say, Stuart or Tudor times, have no idea at all what our forebears looked like, with perhaps the exception of a note in someone's diary or family tradition about isolated characteristics such as hair colour or temper! Today many people struggle to connect with previous generations; we have no way to remember them, to know what they thought and felt, how they lived their lives and worked out their faith, if any; there is no handle to access the past. Jewish tradition is rich with opportunities to connect not just with the past four or five generations, but to connect with our people three and a half thousand years ago as we rehearse each year the Exodus from Egypt, standing at Sinai to receive the *Torah*, God's provision during our years in the wilderness and other formational events in our history. Although we do not know what individual people looked like - after all, the comment that Moshe's face shone after he had been with the Lord doesn't tell us much - we do have a detailed record of the life events that they experienced and can read quite a few of their emotions between the lines of the narratives.

More critically for us as believers in Messiah Yeshua, how do we remember and connect with Him? How do we link into His words and teaching so that He is a reality in our lives, not just the blond-haired, blue-eyed, sandal-wearing man in the sparkling white robe and blue scarf that can be seen in thousands of churches around the world? Our own sense tell us that those pictures must be wrong - Yeshua would almost certainly have had the characteristic Mediterranean dark if not black hair, dark brown eyes and olive skin colour and after days on the road, his cloak would certainly have lost that freshly laundered look, if it had ever been white rather than natural flax or linen colour. The Gospels are completely silent about Yeshua's physical appearance; not a hint escapes through the evangelists' writing - we know absolutely nothing unique or particular about His physical appearance. This is, of course, absolutely in keeping with the commandment: "You shall not make for yourselves idols, nor shall you set up for yourselves an image or a sacred pillar, nor shall you place a figured stone in your land to bow down to it; for I am the Lord your God" (Vayikra 26:1, NASB), but it frustrates our human desire to connect with someone we want to know and love.

God has of course provided the answer. Two answers in fact. Firstly, we remember Yeshua in the way that He told us to remember Him: "And when He had taken some bread and given thanks, He broke it, and gave it to them, saying, 'This is My body which is given for you; do this in remembrance of Me'" (Luke 22:19, NASB). As we celebrate communion, by sharing the Lord's Table - however and whenever this is done in our particular tradition - we remember who He is and what He has done for us; we anchor our faith in a practical act of remembrance. Secondly, we remember Yeshua in each other, loving and sharing with each other as He did the first disciples. By this too we fulfill His words: "By this is My Father glorified, that you bear much fruit, and so prove to be My disciples" (John 15:8, NASB). Whether we are Jews, also celebrating the feasts a reminder of God's continued faithfulness and covenant with our people, or Gentiles grafted into the family of Abraham by faith, our connection to Yeshua becomes alive by our rehearsal and enactment of His words at that last *Pesach seder* before He gave Himself for us: the Lamb of God who takes away the sin of the world.

Further Study: 1 Samuel 7:12-13; 1 Corinthians 4:17

Application: If you are tempted to despair that you can't connect with Yeshua, that He is just too remote for you to know, why not revisit His words and find comfort in remembering Him as He instructed. You're not attending a funeral but a glorious celebration of freedom and intimacy as we eat from His hands and share His cup. Sing, shout, dance, whoop for joy, for our redemption has arrived!

פִּינְחָס ז׳

Pinkhas - Pinchas - 7

B'Midbar / Numbers 29:12 - 30:1

B'Midbar/Numbers 29:12 And on the fifteenth day of the seventh month, there shall be for you a holy assembly ...

וּבַחֲמִשָּׁה עָשָׂר יוֹם לַחֹדֶשׁ הַשְּׁבִיעִי
hash'viyiy lakhodesh yom   asar oova'khamisha
מִקְרָא־קֹדֶשׁ יִהְיֶה לָכֶם
lachem yih'yeh kodesh   mikra

Chapter 29 of B'Mibdar contains the detailed description of the offerings to be made during the block of holy days that are known as the Autumn or Fall Feasts: *Yom Teruah*, *Yom Kippur*, *Sukkot* and *Shemini Atzeret*. The first four verses of the seventh *aliyah* form one of the festival readings that is read on the first day of *Sukkot*, the seven-day festival that starts on the fifteenth day of the month of Tishrei: the seventh month of the religious year, the first month of the civil year. At that point, the reading seems odd because although it is formally two weeks into the new year, it is nevertheless counted as being at the end of the previous year's reading cycle - followed by the seldom read portion *V'Zot HaBracha* (D'varim chapters 33 and 34) - before the new year's cycle starts with B'resheet between seven and fourteen days later.

Whereas the instructions for the feast of *Sukkot* in Vayikra focus on the building of the *sukkah* and the waving of the *lulav* and *etrog*, the instructions here are entirely concerned with the extra sacrifices and offerings to be brought into the sanctuary. As well as the regular offerings, each day of *Sukkot* saw two rams, fourteen year-old male lambs and a male goat - together with their matching grain and drink offerings. The variable part of the sacrifices was the number of young bulls to be sacrificed each day, starting with thirteen on the first day, decreasing by one each day to seven on the last day. A total of seventy young bulls throughout the week. Ancient commentators have long dubbed *Sukkot* as the Feast of the Nations or the Feast of the Gentiles, aligning the seventy bulls with the seventy proto-nations catalogued in B'resheet chapter 10 as the descendants of Noah's three sons, Ham, Shem and Japheth. "R. Eleazar stated, To what do those seventy bullocks correspond? To the seventy nations" (*b. Sukkah 55b*). *Midrash Tanchuma* goes further and asserts that the bullocks were offered as an atonement for the sins of the nations (*Midrash Tanchuma: Pinchas*). Israel acts as "a kingdom of priests" (Shemot 19:6) for the nations of the world, offering sacrifices for the nations each year at *Sukkot*.

The *haftarah* reading for *Sukkot*, from the last chapter of the prophet Zechariah, connects the nations and the Feast of *Sukkot* again. In the Last Days, the prophet says, the nations will come up against Jerusalem for war, so that *HaShem* Himself will fight for His nation, leading to a time when "Adonai will be king over the whole world. On that day Adonai will be the only one, and His name will be the only name" (Zechariah 14:9, CJB) quoted in the *Aleinu* prayer every day in the synagogue. Jerusalem will be restored and rebuilt so that finally, "everyone remaining from all the nations that came to attack Yerushalayim will go up every year to worship the king, Adonai-Tzva'ot [the Lord of Hosts], and to keep the festival of Sukkot" (v. 16, CJB).

But the rabbinic understanding of these texts and the prophecy of Zechariah were to follow many years after *HaShem's* instructions to Moshe and the people of Israel were originally given. The people were still in the desert, still waiting to enter the Promised Land. What could they have made of these instructions? Certainly the *Torah* tells us in just a couple of chapters' time that some of the tribes had many animals: "The descendants of Re'uven and the descendants of Gad had vast quantities of livestock" (B'Midbar 32:1, CJB), so much so that they wanted to settle east of the Jordan river in the land of Gilead which was flat and good for livestock. But to sacrifice seventy bulls in just one week? Why did God ordain these sacrifices, which could not be carried out until the people were settled in the Land and the Tabernacle or Temple were established?

Like much of the *Torah*, which was also contingent upon being in the Land and having a central sanctuary where the priests and Levites would maintain the daily and annual cycles of sacrifice and worship, these instructions provided the certainty of a future and a purpose. This was not just for the current generation, to inspire or motivate them to hold on to God and His promises and to enter the Land; neither was it just for their children, to provide an incentive for conquering the Land, pushing back the pagan nations destined for destruction. These instructions provided a multi-generational vision of service and witness to the nations of the world, a purpose that - although they did not know it - would span centuries and millenia reaching down to the days of Messiah and beyond, through the years of the church age and the times of the Gentiles until the Last Days in which we now live.

Peter, writing to "God's chosen people, living as aliens in the Diaspora"

(1 Peter 1:1, CJB), reminds the early Jewish believers that their role as "a chosen people, the King's cohanim, a holy nation, a people for God to possess" (2:9, CJB) has not ended but continues as the Gentiles are called to stand alongside the Jewish people to share the good news of the Messiah among all the nations. Now atonement for every man, woman and child is guaranteed in and through the blood of Messiah, shed on the stake at Calvary. The agents of delivery, the means that God is using to convey that message of reconciliation to the world, remain the Jewish people who will be a witness for Him forever, aided and assisted by the Gentiles who have come to believe in Yeshua and the God of Israel. While Jew and Gentile alike share the good news **"to the Jew first and also to the Greek"** (Romans 1:16, NASB), the Jewish people as a corporate whole, as a set-apart and holy nation, remain God's witness to the nations of the world and a standard by which they will be held accountable. Their longevity and continued existence, language and culture after nearly 2,000 years out of their Land and dispersed among the often hostile nations of the world is a testimony to Rav Sha'ul's assertion that "From the standpoint of the gospel they are enemies for your sake, but from the standpoint of God's choice they are beloved for the sake of the fathers; for the gifts and the calling of God are irrevocable" (Romans 11:28-29, NASB).

So for us today, whether Jew or Gentile, as believers in Messiah Yeshua, God's purpose continues to be worked out in our midst. The prophet Isaiah spoke beforehand about Messiah's suffering: "I gave My back to those who strike Me, and My cheeks to those who pluck out the beard; I did not cover My face from humiliation and spitting" (Isaiah 50:6, NASB); words that were chillingly fulfilled by the Roman and Jewish authorities. Rav Sha'ul speaks of the same treatment as messenger of the gospel: "Till this very moment we go hungry and thirsty, we are dressed in rags, we are treated roughly, we wander from place to place, we exhaust ourselves working with our own hands for our living. When we are cursed, we keep on blessing; when we are persecuted, we go on putting up with it; when we are slandered, we continue making our appeal. We are the world's garbage, the scum of the earth - yes, to this moment!" (1 Corinthians 4:11-13, CJB). The mere fact that it continues shows us that we are still engaged in mortal combat for the souls of the world, partnering with God who does not want to give up on anyone (2 Peter 3:9). Indeed, should this not be the case, we should question whether we are still in the centre of God's will for us and for these days. "Beloved, do not be surprised at the fiery ordeal among you, which comes upon you for your testing, as though some strange thing were happening to you; but to the degree that you share the sufferings of Messiah, keep on rejoicing; so that also at the revelation of His glory, you may rejoice with exultation" (1 Peter 4:12-13, NASB).

Further Study: 1 Corinthians 2:6-9; Daniel 11:33-35; Psalm 66:8-10

Application: Do you know and walk in God's purpose for your life? Is the certainty of your calling tested on a daily basis? Whilst we should not seek persecution, its presence confirms that we are still a threat to the enemy and so serving God.

מַטּוֹת / מַסְעֵי

Mattot - Tribes / Masa'ei - Stages

B'Midbar / Numbers 30:2 - 36:13

- in leap years, the two parashiyot are read separately; in regular years, they are read together -

רִאשׁוֹן	Aliyah One	B'Midbar/Numbers 30:2 - 31:12
שְׁלִישִׁי	Aliyah Three	B'Midbar/Numbers 32:1 - 19
רְבִיעִי	Aliyah Four	B'Midbar/Numbers 32:20 - 33:49
שִׁשִּׁי	Aliyah Six	B'Midbar/Numbers 34:16 - 35:8
שְׁבִיעִי	Aliyah Seven	B'Midbar/Numbers 35:9 - 36:13

מַטּוֹת - B'Midbar/Numbers 30:2 - 32:42

שֵׁנִי	Aliyah Two	B'Midbar/Numbers 31:1 - 12
חֲמִישִׁי	Aliyah Five	B'Midbar/Numbers 31:42 - 54

מַסְעֵי - B'Midbar/Numbers 33:1 - 36:13

שֵׁנִי	Aliyah Two	B'Midbar/Numbers 33:11 - 49
חֲמִישִׁי	Aliyah Five	B'Midbar/Numbers 35:1 - 8

מַטּוֹת / מַסְעֵי א׳

Mattot - Tribes / Masa'ei - Stages - 1

(In a leap year this could be read as Mattot 1)

B'Midbar / Numbers 30:2 - 31:12

B'Midbar/Numbers 30:2 So Moshe spoke to the heads of the tribes of the Children of Israel

וַיְדַבֵּר מֹשֶׁה אֶל־רָאשֵׁי הַמַּטּוֹת לִבְנֵי
liv'ney   ha'mattot   roshey   el   Moshe   vay'dabeyr

יִשְׂרָאֵל
Yisrael

    Rashi comments that Moshe accorded honour to the princes or heads of the twelve tribes by teaching them first before going on to teach all the Children of Israel afterwards. Rashi asserts that all the *Torah* was taught this way: first to the leaders and then to the people, and he quotes the incident of Moshe's face shining when he came down from Mt. Sinai with the second set of tablets: "Then Moshe called to them and Aharon and all the rulers in the congregation returned to him; and Moshe spoke to them. And afterwards, all the sons of Israel came near, and he commanded them to do everything that the Lord had spoken to him on Mount Sinai" (Shemot 34:31-32, NASB).

    Teaching the leaders first was not only a matter of honour and public relations, however. It was also an important demonstration of how *Torah* was to be preserved and taught from generation to generation. Moshe modelled the process that would be needed to make sure that the message was successfully and correctly passed on. The leaders were known and trusted by the men of their own tribes, so Moshe taught them (who all knew him) first, then taught the people when the people could see their leaders agreeing with what he said, and the leaders could be responsible for follow-up explanations and confirmation once the initial teaching was done.

    We find Rav Sha'ul teaching the same principle to Timothy when he writes, "And the things which you have heard from me in the presence of many witnesses, these entrust to faithful men, who will be able to teach others also" (2 Timothy 2:2, NASB). Rav Sha'ul is urging Timothy to teach faithful men -

"trustworthy" as another translation has it - who will in turn teach others so that the teaching passes on through reliable people.

Of course, this also follows the teaching of the Master Himself. "Therefore, go and make people from all nations into talmidim ... teaching them to obey everything that I have commanded you" (Matthew 28:19-20, CJB) were Yeshua's words to whom? To the people of Israel? No, to His particular disciples, His chosen leaders who were to spread the gospel to the whole of Israel and to the world beyond.

Further Study: Jeremiah 35:6-10,18-19; Ezra 7:25-25

Application: As leaders, teachers or parents - all engaged in passing on the tradition of faith to the next generation of physical or spiritual disciples - we need to follow the Master's methods.

מַטּוֹת ב׳

Mattot - Tribes - 2

(In an ordinary year this could be read as Mattot/Masa'ei 1)

B'Midbar / Numbers 31:1 - 12

B'Midbar/Numbers 31:2 Take vengeance for the Children of Israel from the Midianites

נְקֹם נִקְמַת בְּנֵי יִשְׂרָאֵל מֵאֵת הַמִּדְיָנִים
ha'Midyaniym mey'eyt Yisra'el b'ney nik'mat n'kom

Both the first words in the text are derived from the same root: נָקַם, which is normally translated as taking revenge or vengeance. When the Hebrew text uses this technique: combining a verb and noun from the same root - and we see other examples over swearing oaths and dreaming dreams - it is always used as a device for sharp emphasis, something that English finds difficult to do in the same way. How are we going to understand such a strong command to take vengeance alongside such equally strong commands in the opposite direction: "You shall not take vengeance" (Vayikra 19:18, NASB), "Vengeance is Mine, I will repay" (D'varim 32:35, NIV). Is there a measure of contradiction going on here?

Jacob Milgrom says that the word נָקַם should not be translated as 'avenge' or 'revenge' but redressing past wrongs or exacting retribution; in other words, that there is an element of justice involved: it should not be seen as mean-spirited "getting back" at people who have wronged us but a necessary corrective to re-instate the situation that prevailed before the initial offence. Rabbi Samson Racphael Hirsch goes even further: pointing to the possibility that נָקַם may be a reflexive derivative of the verb קוּם, to arise, he suggests that it may be translated as "rise up for yourselves". He goes on to draw a distinction between the Moabites, who wanted to destroy the Israelites physically so as to expel them from their land, and the Midianites, who wanted to destroy the Israelites at a spiritual level - by involving them in idolatry - so that they would cease to be a light and witness to the nations for God. So Hirsch projects this command as being an essential step to extract the Israelites from under the spiritual influence of the Midianites, pointing to the word מֵאֵת: the Midyanites are not just the direct object of the vengeance, but including the preposition מִן, from, there is a sense of movement away from Midyanite control or influence. So there may be occasions when it is right to remove ourselves from a harmful or controlling situation, using forceful means if necessary to ensure separation. The Psalmist wrote, "The righteous rejoice to see vengeance done" (Psalm 58:11, CJB). It is a good thing when people are able to find freedom from situations and behaviour patterns that are stunting their spiritual growth.

How do we do this today as followers of Messiah Yeshua? Rav Sha'ul wrote: "Repay no one evil for evil, but try to do what everyone regards as good. If possible, and to the extent that it depends on you, live in peace with all people. Never seek revenge, my friends; instead leave that to God's anger ... if your enemy is hungry, feed him; if he is thirsty, give him something to drink" (Romans 12:17-20, CJB).

Further Study: Jeremiah 51:11-12; Ezekiel 25:12-17; Matthew 5:38-48

Application: At a human level, it is very easy to think thoughts of revenge and retribution on those who we think or feel have wronged us, and sometimes all too easy to carry them out. Recognising that no-one is meant to suffer abusive situations, we should "rise up for ourselves" and show God's love in a firm and open-handed way.

מַטּוֹת 'ה

Mattot - Tribes - 5

(In an ordinary year this could be read as Mattot/Masa'ei 2)

B'Midbar / Numbers 31:42 - 54

B'Midbar/Numbers 31:50 And we have brought the offering of Adonai ... to atone for our souls before Adonai.

וַנַּקְרֵב אֶת־קָרְבַּן יהוה ... לְכַפֵּר
l'chapeyr ... Adonai korban et vanak'reyv
עַל־נַפְשֹׁתֵינוּ לִפְנֵי יהוה:
Adonai lifney nafshoteynu al

How can this offering - the gold from the officers' share of the booty from the destruction of the Midianites - bring atonement, and why was atonement required? This verse follows the account of the successful battle when although many Midianites were killed, it was at the Lord's instruction, so surely no atonement was necessary on that account. Sforno answers the question this way: "because we did not protest about the sinners at Pe'or"; he suggests that the atonement was necessary because the officers had failed to protest about - and therefore prevent - the sins of the people with the Midianite women, worshipping their idol; and if there had been a protest and so no sin, the destruction of the Midianites might not have been necessary. Hirsch, commenting on the phrase קָרְבַּן יהוה - the offering of *Adonai* - points out that because the text says "the offering of *Adonai*" rather than "an offering to *Adonai*", this offering is being brought as a duty to thank God for preservation and protection; the lives of the officers and the men had all been saved, thus an atonement offering was due. In similar vein, highlighting that the officers had had to count all the fighting men to be sure that everyone was present and accounted for, Milgrom suggests that this was a counting and census issue: "When you take a census of the sons of Israel to number them, then each one of them shall give a ransom for himself to the Lord, when you number them, that there may be no plague among them when you number them" (Shemot 30:12, NASB); as the officers had counted, they brought an offering from their booty to atone for the lives of both themselves and the men whom they had counted to see that no-one was missing.

Rashi and the Sages of the Talmud, on the other hand, present an entirely different answer. Rashi, in his usual laconic style simply says: "to atone for our thoughts about the daughters of Midian", while the Talmud constructs a conversation between Moshe and the officers on the subject: "Moshe - Why an atonement? Officers - Though we escaped from sin, yet we did not escape from meditating upon sin. So straightaway we brought the Lord's offering" (*b. Shabbat* 64a). The *Midrash* is even more explicit: when they had stripped the Midianite women of the ornaments and jewelry, some from intimate places, they did not violate their bodies - "Nevertheless, not one of us was joined with one of them in this world, so as not to be joined with her in Gehenna in the world to come. May this stand up in our favour on the day of Great Judgement, to make atonement for us before the Lord" (*Targum Neofiti*). In these days of warfare when soldiers are being accused of unethical behaviour, raping and abusing civilians in Iraq - simply another episode among many in the sad history of war and soldiers throughout the ages taking advantage of the civilian population - it is significant that the behaviour of the Israelite army here was almost unique: they did not sexually abuse the women. It is also worth pointing out that the behaviour of IDF soldiers today towards Arab women is similarly exemplary with almost no cases of rape or abuse being credibly reported in spite of the IDF's command structure being rigorous to investigate any such claims quickly and thoroughly.

What is interesting is the reason the *Targum* provides for this behaviour: no man wanted to be joined in this world - and so also in the next - with a woman who would be sent to Gehenna because of her life of idolatry and, now, attempting to buy her life with sex. This bears a striking connection to Yeshua's words about marriage: "For this reason a man should leave his father and mother and be united with his wife, and the two are to become one flesh. Thus they are no longer two but one. So then, no-one should break apart what God has joined together" (Mark 10:7-9, CJB). Intercourse is one of three ways that the rabbis consider a marriage to be contracted, so the writers of the *midrash* saw not only the Israelite man becoming permanently linked in this world to a Midianite woman if he had sexual intercourse with her (be that rape or consensual), but that the tie between the two would endure into the next world, with the Israelite man being dragged down to share her punishment for idolatry. Whether this was thought to be simply because of the link itself, or because her subsequent behaviour, sin and further idolatry, would cause him too to sin is unclear. We do know that Moshe taught the people: "Be careful, after [the nations of the Land] have been destroyed ahead of you, not to be trapped into following them; so that you enquire after their gods and ask, 'How did these nations serve their gods? I want to do the same'" (D'varim 12:30, CJB).

Rav Sha'ul picks up the same theme when he writes to the Corinthians. Corinth was a sea port and a cultic centre, so well supplied with prostitutes of every kind, and Sha'ul vividly highlights the issue: "Don't you know that your bodies are part of the Messiah? So, am I to take parts of the Messiah and make them parts of a prostitute? Heaven forbid! Don't you know that a man who joins himself to a prostitute becomes physically one with her? For the Tanakh says, 'The two will become one flesh'" (1 Corinthians 6:15-16, CJB). Sha'ul sees this physical link as having great spiritual strength, creating a bond that damages the believer. He goes on: "Run from sexual immorality! Every other sin a person commits is outside the body, but the fornicator sins against his own body" (v. 18, CJB). Sexual sin is something that affects us right inside; the way that pornography becomes an addiction is a modern proof of this old truth. As Rav Sha'ul concludes, "Your body is a temple for the Ruach HaKodesh who lives inside you, whom you received from God? The fact is, you don't belong to yourselves, for you were bought at a price. So use your bodies to glorify God" (vv. 19-20, CJB). Sha'ul's words apply equally to men and women, for either gender may entrap or be entrapped in sexual sin.

Further Study: Jeremiah 1:1-5; Romans 12:2; 1 Corinthians 8:12

Application: How do you use your body and body language? Do you dress modestly and carefully so as to protect yourself and others not just from sin but from meditating upon sin? Each of us has a responsibility not only for ourselves but the effect that we might have on others. As Yeshua said, "Whoever causes one of these ... who believe in Me to stumble, it would be better to be tied to a millstone and thrown into the sea" (Mark 9:42).

מַטּוֹת / מַסְעֵי 'ג

Mattot - Tribes / Masa'ei - Stages - 3

(In a leap year this could be read as Mattot 6)

B'Midbar / Numbers 32:1 - 19

B'Midbar/Numbers 32:1 There was great wealth to the sons of R'uvein and to the sons of Gad, exceedingly numerous.

וּמִקְנֶה רַב הָיָה לִבְנֵי רְאוּבֵן וְלִבְנֵי־גָד עָצוּם
atzum Gad v'livney R'uveyn livney hayah rav oomikneh

מְאֹד
m'od

While all the tribes of Israel kept cattle, Reuben and Gad were cattle ranchers par excellence; they were the cattle barons of their time and God had blessed them abundantly in cattle and sheep. As they looked at the size of their flocks and herds, plus of course those of the other tribes, they couldn't help feeling a certain unease: where were all these animals going to go? They remembered how Avraham and his nephew Lot had had to part company because their flocks and herds became too great and all the trouble that had caused; just their animals alone must be many more than Avraham had by himself, so where were the other tribes going? Was the Land going to be big enough for all that grazing? As they pondered this, their eyes couldn't help looking around at the plains of Moab, where Israel had only just conquered the kingdoms of Sichon and Og and taken possession of their lands and cities. An idea started to form - why shouldn't they have this land here on the east of the Jordan: miles and miles of open country, plenty of grazing land, water and cities to live in; that would leave plenty of space west of the Jordan for the other tribes. Perfect!

Later history tells us that this was not a popular idea among the other tribes and led to more than a certain amount of angst over the years. The river Jordan was a much more defensible boundary than an arbitrary line drawn somewhere in the wilderness. Hindsight enables us to see that Reuben and Gad went for the immediate solution that was in front of their eyes, rather than waiting for what God has originally said and planned. They chose by what they saw, according to what they had now, rather than holding on and waiting for God's plans to be worked out in detail. Rabbi Hirsch even suggests that the idea of settling by themselves within special boundaries outside those of the general nation appealed to them.

Yeshua tells a parable about a rich man who had very productive land, producing much more grain than he had the capacity to store. The man said to himself, "I will tear down my barns and build larger ones, and there I will store all my grain and my goods ... take your ease, eat, drink and be merry" (Luke 12:18-19, NASB). But God had other ideas and the man's planning was wasted. Yeshua goes on to teach that "your Father knows that you need these things. But seek for His kingdom and these things shall be added to you" (vv. 30-31, NASB).

Rav Sha'ul picks up the same theme writing to the Corinthians. Talking about the difference between our earthly existence here and being with God in the time to come he says, "for we walk by faith, not by sight" (2 Corinthians 5:7, ESV). Sometimes we have to ignore what we see and trust that what God has said He is going to do. "Faith assures us of things we expect and convinces us of the existence of things we cannot see" (Hebrews 11:1, GWT).

Further Study: Romans 8:22-25; 2 Corinthians 4:16-18; 1 Peter 1:8-9

Application: Are you trying to take important decisions at the moment and finding it difficult to balance the seeming certainties of what you see against the promises that God has given you but seem a long time coming? Don't let the enemy rush you into making a snap decision based on here and now and so deprive you of God's blessing. Hold on until you are sure it is God and then make your move.

מַטּוֹת / מַסְעֵי ד׳

Mattot - Tribes / Masa'ei - Stages - 4

(In a leap year this could be read as Mattot 7)

B'Midbar / Numbers 32:20 - 33:49

B'Midbar/Numbers 32:20 ... if you will arm yourselves before the Lord for the battle ...

אִם־תֵּחָלְצוּ לִפְנֵי יהוה לַמִּלְחָמָה:
lamil'hamah Adonai lifney teykhal'tzu im

The verb תֵּחָלְצוּ is a *Niphal*, prefix, 2mp form of the root חָלַץ. The prefix form usually indicates future or incomplete action, and the *Niphal* stem of this verb means "to get ready for or arm oneself"; here that is qualified by the following לַמִּלְחָמָה, "for battle or fighting". The men of Gad and Reuben, who wanted to be allocated the wide pasture lands east of the Jordan and start farming straight away - for they had many flocks and cattle - were being challenged by Moshe to fully participate in the conquest of the Land of Canaan and not just settle for the low hanging fruit, leaving the rest of the work to others. The modern Hebrew word from the same root - חֲלוּצִים, pioneers - is used to describe the intrepid settlers of the young *Yishuv* in the early years of the 20th century who drained the swamps and started to make the desert bloom even before the founding of the State of Israel. They fought the mosquitos and the malaria and epitomised our text as the JPS Tanakh translates it: "if you go to battle as shock-troops, at the instance of the Lord" (JPS).

The Ba'al HaTurim points out that the qualifying phrase "before the Lord" occurs seven times in the following verses - 20, 21, 22 (twice), 27, 29 and 32 - to correspond with the seven years that the conquest of the Land would take. This emphasises that the men of Gad and Reuben were taking on a commitment before *HaShem* to serve alongside the other tribes for the duration of the campaign, in order to be allocated their land now so that their women and children could be settled and start farming in the land conquered from the Amorites east of the Jordan. It also makes an important point that cuts several ways concerning the battles that we fight: firstly, that in order to take ground for the Kingdom of God, warfare is required - it is necessary to fight; secondly, that we are required to arm ourselves - we have to take an active part in the process and cannot just sit and wait for things to fall into our laps; thirdly, that we arm ourselves "before the Lord" or according to His instructions - we are only to fight the battles that He calls us into and on the terms that He sets out for us.

Many believers today are uncomfortable with the idea of physical conflict, believing that Yeshua was a pacifist. David Bivin summarises these ideas: "Here was a man who apparently was willing to die rather than defend Himself, a man who taught His disciples not to kill, not to resist evil, to love their enemies, not to fear those who kill the body, and that only those who are willing to lose their lives will be able to save them (Matthew 5:21,39a,44; 10:28; 16:25)." Yet as Bivin goes on to point out, Sha'ul tells us to "hate what is evil" (Romans 12:9) and James adds, "Resist the devil" (James 4:7). Luke's gospel makes it clear that Yeshua's disciples were armed (Luke 22:38, 49), while Yeshua Himself told the disciples, "let him who has no sword sell his robe and buy one" (Luke 22:36, NASB).

Rav Sha'ul extends this to the spiritual plane to make sure that we understand the principles involved: "Use all the armour and weaponry that God provides, so that you will be able to stand against the deceptive tactics of the Adversary. For we are not struggling against human beings, but against the rulers, authorities and cosmic powers governing this darkness, against the spiritual forces of evil in the heavenly realms" (Ephesians 6:11-12, CJB). The fight that we fight is not necessarily against people - although many of us may be involved in physical war or service in the armed forces of the countries in which we live - because the real enemy, the real battle, is a spiritual one, against the devil and his hordes who seek to destroy all that God is doing and push back the advances of the Kingdom of God. Sha'ul goes on, to illustrate the need for our active participation: "So take up every piece of war equipment that God provides; so that when the evil day comes, you will be able to resist; and when the battle is won, you will be standing" (v. 13 CJB). Whatever resources God provides are of no use whatsoever unless we pick them up, put them on and use them. Sha'ul also makes it clear that we haven't just signed up for a skirmish or two, if it is conveniently located or forced upon us, but that just like the men of Gad and Reuben, we are committed for the long haul, to see the job done and the battle won.

Further Study: Nehemiah 4:7-8(13-14); 1 Peter 5:8-11

Application: It is inevitable as believers that we will be involved in conflict as the enemy tries to thwart the plans of God in our lives and in the wider world. The question we have to answer is whether we will resist the enemy, making use of all that God has given us - be that in the (appropriate) physical or the spiritual realm - or whether we simply allow the enemy to walk all over us. What will your decision be today?

מַסְעֵי ב'

Masa'ei - Stages -2

(In an ordinary year this could be read as Mattot/Masa'ei 4)

B'midbar / Numbers 33:11 - 49

B'midbar/Numbers 33:18 They travelled from Hazeroth and camped in Ritmah.

וַיִּסְעוּ מֵחֲצֵרוֹת וַיַּחֲנוּ בְּרִתְמָה:

b'Ritmah   vayakhanu meyKhatzeyrot vayis'u

Rashi explains why this particular stop on our peoples' journey through the desert has this name. The word רִתְמָה, meaning 'broom' or 'juniper', is the noun derived from the root verb רָתַם which means to bind, yoke or harness. The narrative at B'Midbar 12:16 and 13:3 tell us that it was at the camping place after Hazeroth that the spies were sent out to reconnoitre the Land and came back with a bad report; believing it, the people became bound, so that in a sense, the place name can mean "the binding".

Rashi also connects the name to Psalm 120:3-4 where a deceitful tongue is allied to burning coals from a broom or juniper tree. Unlike other coals, the juniper continues to burn on the inside, even though the outside has cooled and gone black - so it is easy to inadvertently get burned by touching or picking up juniper coals that look spent and cold. So it is with gossip and slander: even though apparently forgiven, they can be held in someone's heart and then flare up to cause damage later (cf. B'resheet Rabbah 98:19).

Yeshua's *talmidim* were having some trouble understanding just what that might mean, so one of the most frequent spokesmen - Peter - came to Yeshua and asked Him, "how often can my brother sin against me and I have to forgive him? As many as seven times?" (Matthew 18:21, CJB). Peter thought he was setting a pretty high limit; after all, if someone repeats the same offence seven times, even if they say 'Sorry' in between, they must seem very determined to offend and not very sincere in their apologies. "'No, not seven times,' answered Yeshua, 'but seventy times seven!'" (v. 22, CJB).

Yeshua names an impossibly high number - 490 times - but you would have lost count way before you got there, so it effectively means: without number, always. Yeshua then goes on to tell the parable of the slave who owes an enormous sum of money to a king, who recognising that the debt is unpayable, has compassion on the slave and forgives the debt. The slave, however, then has a fellow slave thrown into jail over a much smaller sum and when the king hears about it, he has the first slave thrown into prison and re-instates the debt, rebuking him for showing no mercy when he had been shown so much himself. Yeshua emphasises that forgiveness is a chain process - it is passed on from person to person, as He taught in the Lord's Prayer: "forgive us our trespasses as we forgive them that trespass against us" (6:12, BCP[12]).

The final phrase of Yeshua's parable brings us round full circle to where we started: "This is how My heavenly Father will treat you, unless you each forgive your brother from your hearts" (18:35, CJB). Our forgiveness must be complete and from our hearts so that we don't burn on like the juniper coals.

Further Study: Zechariah 7:8-14; Ephesians 4:31-32

Application: How is your forgiveness? Is there someone that you need to forgive from your heart so as to release the binding for both of you? Remember, forgiveness on the surface leaves the hurt in place, ready to flare up and bite you later.

---

12. Book of Common Prayer, 1662

מַטּוֹת / מַסְעֵי׳

Mattot - Tribes / Masa'ei - Stages - 6

(In a leap year this could be read as Masa'ei 4)

B'Midbar / Numbers 34:16 - 35:8

B'Midbar/Numbers 34:17 These are the names of the men who will take possession of the land for you ...

אֵלֶּה שְׁמוֹת הָאֲנָשִׁים אֲשֶׁר־יִנְחֲלוּ לָכֶם
lachem yin'khalu asher ha'anashim sh'mot eyleh

אֶת־הָאָרֶץ
ha'aretz et

The verb in the text, יִנְחֲלוּ, is a *Qal* 3mp prefix form from the root נָחַל. Davidson lists three overlapping meanings: to obtain, acquire a possession, to possess; to obtain by inheritance, to inherit; to divide for a possession, to apportion. נָחַל is routinely used to describe the process of inheritance, from one generation to another, of taking possession of an inheritance, and the noun נַחֲלָה is translated as a possession, property or estate, an inheritance, portion or lot. We can see all three meanings at work in our text. The men that Moshe was instructed to select were to lead the tribes in taking physical possession of the Land; they were also to take up the inheritance of the Land that *HaShem* had promised to Avraham, Yitz'khak and Ya'akov; finally, they were to be involved in the allotting of the inheritance portions to the clans, families and individuals within their tribes. Friedman makes the comment that, "Over and over, the tribes and their leaders are named in this book of the *Torah*. From the wilderness period to the times of the judges to the time of the monarchy, Israel is never ruled by an individual political authority. There are always tribal chiefs, councils of leaders, priests, judges and military officers."

Rashi comments on the word לָכֶם, which would normally be translated "for you" or "to you" and suggests that here it should be rendered "on your behalf" or "on your account". He explains that the tribal leaders were acting as representatives, rather than principles; they were receiving the inheritance on behalf of the people, rather than dividing it between them. Quoting "יהוה יִלָּחֵם לָכֶם - HaShem will do battle or fight for you" (Shemot 14:14) as another example, Rashi points out that *HaShem* defeated the army of the Egyptians on behalf of Israel; they were not capable of fighting, so He fought in their place. He did what they could not do.

Rabbi Hirsch is even more definite: "the prince of every tribe is to 'take into possession' on behalf of his tribe, the portion of land allocated to it, and make the sub-division amongst the families and men who are entitled thereto." He sees the leaders as appointed representatives having full authority "to act for all claims of heritage, and their decisions are legally and finally binding." Hirsch points out that the Sages of the Talmud use this verse as the basis for the *halacha* that if a court appoints guardians to look after the estate of minors, then when the children reach their majority, they are not allowed to protest against the management of their estate because the guardians were appointed by the court so acted with the court's authority (*b. Kiddushin* 42a). The court intended to act in the interest of the minors to protect their inheritance, so appointed guardians to administer the estate on their behalf.

Is this perhaps the idea that Rav Sha'ul had in mind when he wrote: "But God demonstrates His own love for us in that the Messiah died on our behalf while we were still sinners" (Romans 5:8, CJB). Knowing that we were powerless, being in effect His enemies because of sin, God appointed His Son to take the punishment of our sin "on our behalf" or "in our place". "He made Him who knew no sin to be sin on our behalf, that we might become the righteousness of God in Him" (2 Corinthians 5:21, NASB). God Himself decided what to do and then - in Messiah Yeshua - took the necessary action. His decision cannot be argued with or disputed; it is completely final, as the apostles explained: "And there is salvation in no one else; for there is no other name under heaven that has been given among men, by which we must be saved" (Acts 4:12, NASB).

This idea does not always sit easily with man. Only weeks earlier, Yeshua and the *talmidim* had assembled for their *Pesach seder*. Before the meal started, Yeshua "rose from the table, removed His outer garments and wrapped a towel around His waist. Then He poured some water into a basin and began to wash the feet of the talmidim and wipe them off with the towel wrapped around Him" (John 13:4-5, CJB). "Just a minute," Peter objects, "what do you think you're doing? You're not washing my feet!" This is not fair, not appropriate, not going to happen. No way! It was Peter who had spoken the words earlier in Yeshua's ministry that confessed Him as the Messiah, the Son of God. It could never be that the Messiah should wash Peter's feet. Yeshua tried to reason with him: "You don't understand yet what I am doing, but in time you will understand" (v. 7, CJB). Yeshua had used just about the same logic to His cousin John the Baptist when He came to him at the Jordan to be baptised at the start of His ministry: "Permit it at this time; for in this way it is fitting for us to fulfill all righteousness" (Matthew 3:15, NASB). But Peter persisted: "No! ... You will never wash my feet" (John 13:8a, CJB). Finally, Yeshua has to be more blunt: "If I don't wash you, you have no share with Me" (v. 8b, CJB). What Yeshua is saying is that this is the way that God has chosen to do things and that if Peter isn't prepared to do it that way, then he cannot be a part of what God is doing.

Believers in Messiah are often criticised for being too exclusive. Tolerance is a modern tool that the enemy uses to blur the edges of the gospel by persuading believers not to present the world with the clear choice that God intends. Talk of heaven and hell, of judgement, sin and death, is considered old-fashioned and offensive; it constrains people's lifestyle choices and makes them feel uncomfortable. Worse, is not politically correct. I don't think that Yeshua was too fussed about political correctness, but was intensely concerned about people understanding the real issues of life and death and coming into relationship with Him. John the Baptist said: "Behold the Lamb of God who takes away the sin of the world" (John 1:29). Yeshua told His disciples: "I am the way, and the truth, and the life; no one comes to the Father, but through Me" (John 14:6, NASB). That is the truth, in black and white; take or leave it, but there is no halfway position. Yeshua is the way to our inheritance with God; He is the only way to possess the promises that God has made to us.

Further Study: 1 John 2:13-15; John 6:46

Application: The time has long since passed for wishy-washy mealy-mouthed presentations of the gospel that please no-one; too mild to interest anyone, yet just enough to upset people by being made at all. How can you speak out and be bold in declaring the truth about eternal salvation and finding peace with God? Ask the Architect and Designer to show you His plans and tell you when to start shouting!

מַסְעֵי ה'

Masa'ei - Stages - 5

(In an ordinary year this could be read as Mattot/Masa'ei 6)

B'midbar / Numbers 35:1 - 8

B'midbar/Numbers 35:2 cities for dwelling and open space for the cities around them ...

עָרִים לָשֶׁבֶת וּמִגְרָשׁ לֶעָרִים סְבִיבֹתֵיהֶם

s'vivoteyhem   le'ariym   oomigrash   lashavet   ariym

    These are the cities, forty-eight in all, where the Levites are to live among the other tribes of Israel. They are to be given from the land holdings of the other tribes in proportion to the amount of land allocated to each tribe, and include the six cities of refuge, three on each side of the Jordan river. Although the sizes of the cities themselves are not specified, the text does go on to measure the size of the open space that is to come as part of the city's endowment: "from the wall of the city outward a thousand cubits around" (v. 4, NASB). A cubit is approximately eighteen inches, so this belt or ring is about 500 yards wide, a little more than a quarter of a mile. The next verse goes on to "measure outside the city on the east side two thousand cubits" (v. 5, NASB) and so on for the south, west and north sides, "with the city in the centre ... pasture land for the cities" (v. 5, NASB). Commentators differ as to exactly how the measurements worked: one thousand plus another two thousand, or two thousand in total including the first thousand; whether the area was to be circular or rectangular. However, the picture is clear - an area of at least half a square mile with the city at its centre.

    By definition, the use of the land was controlled. Commenting on the first thousand cubits, Rashi - drawing on the Talmud (*b*. Arachin 33b) - says, "open space: a space, a vacant area - outside the city, around, to be an aesthetic enhancement to the city. They are not permitted to build a house there, nor to plant a vineyard, nor to sow any sowing." The inner ring of land is just to be space, recreational land; it cannot be built on, so the city cannot expand or develop urban sprawl. The word מִגְרָשׁ - from the root גָּרַשׁ, to drive out, expel, divorce - is often translated "pasture land", a place where cattle are driven to graze Davidson. The outer ring of land, although still called מִגְרָשׁ, may be used for vineyards and olive groves, possibly for growing vegetables, herbs and fruit; the Levites received no formal apportionment of land, so farming and production of cereal and large scale crops is effectively prohibited. Milgrom makes two interesting points: firstly, "[a] characteristics of pasture land is that it is common property" - the community owned the land so that it could be shared and used by everyone in contrast to farmland which is owned by individuals; secondly, that the מִגְרָשׁ was legally a part of the city, so that "the city limits, within which a man-slayer was safe from the blood redeemer, was not the city walls but the extent of the pasture."

The Levites led a very different life from the other Israelites: a mixture of restriction and provision. The lived in their own cities in the middle of the territory of the other tribes, surrounded by open space that they could use for some things and not for others, not allowed to work like everyone else so that they were free to teach the people and serve both God and the people in the Temple, not allowed to grow their cities but with their houses protected against being sold permanently away from the community, supported by the tithe of the other tribes but having their own flocks and herds for fresh meat and growing their own fresh fruit and vegetables; a people within a people, an organic part of the whole yet ring-fenced and protected, set apart and chosen by God. Even those confined to the cities of refuge had the freedom of the open space so that they too could have some quality of life and outside activity.

Many people consider that becoming a believer is rather like receiving a life sentence: picking up a whole lifestyle of restrictions and obligations, being told what to do all the time, never being able to have fun and with a whole list of "dos and don'ts" to regulate regulate one's life and get in the way of being normal. Yet believers are surprisingly like the Levites in many ways. We are called to live cheek by jowl with everyone else, in the world but - as Yeshua said - "not of the world, even as I am not of the world" (John 17:16, NASB); rubbing shoulders with and working alongside others - in similar, yet at the same time different because we are working to higher orders, occupations - to put fresh food on the table while relying on the Lord for our long-term provision and existence. Rather than being hemmed in by pressures and stress, we are in a wide open space where every one can see us and approach us without obstacles and hindrances in their paths; we have a view and freedom to move where the enemy of our souls cannot reach us, as Rav Sha'ul wrote: "We have all kinds of troubles, but we are not crushed; we are perplexed, yet not in despair; persecuted, yet not abandoned; knocked down, yet not destroyed" (2 Corinthians 4:8-9, CJB). The highest priority in our lives, the most important thing that we do, is no longer a life of work and daily survival but teaching others about God: His laws and the relationship He offers us in Messiah Yeshua; everything should come second to that, for that is why we exist. The resources of the kingdom are at our disposal as we fulfill our assigned tasks and calling, not just in word - for talk is not only cheap but easily ignored - but in our lives, in the quality and depth of our relationships with others, the way we care and give ourselves to others, hospitality and availability, being there for people.

Like the Levites, this is not a position that we chose or resourced for ourselves; it is God at work through us. The other tribes would not have chosen to give land and cities to the Levites, but God said that it should be so: He made it happen; the world certainly does not owe us a living or want to grant us the space for the Kingdom of Heaven to grow, but God has said that it will be so and - often much more slowly than we would like - He is making it happen. Just like the Levites, we also have to act out our parts in this drama that God has produced; we have to open our homes, change our priorities, make ourselves available, speak out the whispers from the prompt box, meet and care for people where they are. When people enter our space - our lives, our homes - are they aware that the open space and the freedom we have to live lives that are pleasing to God, are a blessing to others and fulfill our own deepest needs? God has said that it should be so and is prepared to make it happen. What are you waiting for?

Further Study: 1 Corinthians 9:10-14;   Galatians 5:1

Application: How are you doing on the availability front? This is something that everyone can do at some level because it is God who works in us as we open up to Him and let Him into our lives. Why not take a few minutes today to ask God what He would like you to do?

מַטּוֹת / מַסְעֵי - 7

Mattot - Tribes / Masa'ei - Stages - 7

(In a leap year this could be read as Masa'ei 6)

B'Midbar / Numbers 35:9 - 36:13

B'Midbar/Numbers 35:13 And the cities that you shall appoint: there shall be six cities of refuge for you.

וְהֶעָרִים אֲשֶׁר תִּתֵּנוּ שֵׁשׁ־עָרֵי מִקְלָט תִּהְיֶינָה
v'he'ariym asher titeynu sheysh arey miklat tih'yeynah

לָכֶם:
lachem

Rashi comments that by this verse - "there shall be six cities of refuge" - qualifies the text in the following verse: "Three cities shall be designated beyond the Jordan, and the other three shall be designated in the land of Canaan" (v. 14, JPS) to mean that all six cities must be set in operation together. Moshe designated three on the east of the Jordan - "Bezer, in the wilderness in the Tableland, belonging to the Reubenites; Ramoth, in Gilead, belonging to the Gadites; and Golan, in Bashan, belonging to the Manassites" (D'varim 4:43, JPS) - before our people entered the Land; Joshua designated the other three after the conquest - "So they set aside Kedesh in the hill country of Naphtali in Galilee, Shechem in the hill country of Ephraim, and Kiriath-arba - that is, Hebron - in the country of Judah" (Joshua 20:7, JPS). Rashi has in mind the passage from the Mishnah where the Sages say, "[they do not afford refuge] until all six of them afford refuge at the same time" (*m. Makkot* 2:4). This is echoed by Rabbi Hirsch, who comments that "the institution of מִקְלָט must come into force simultaneously in the whole Jewish domain" to emphasise that the cities of refuge are available to any inhabitant of the land, be they a native-born Israelite, a convert or a sojourner in the Land (v. 15) if they have killed someone by accident. Some commentators suggest that the verse "And when the Lord your God enlarges your territory ... then you shall add three more towns to those three" (D'varim 19:8-9, JPS) can be read as saying that when the population rises, another three cities should be added to those west of the Jordan.

Rashi is also concerned that the number of cities on each side of the Jordan doesn't seem to match the residential population: "There were nine tribes in the Land of Canaan and here there were only two and a half". The Sages of the Talmud suggested that a disproportionate number of cities were needed on the east because there was a much higher incidence of murder and manslaughter east of the river, citing the text "Gilead is a city of evildoers, tracked up with blood" (Hosea 6:8, JPS) to say "Said Abaye: By reason that manslaying was rife in Gilead" (*b*. Makkot 9*b*). The Ramban, on the the other hand, points out that "the land of the [east] side of the Jordan was a very large land and required three cities of refuge just as the whole Land of Israel on the [west] side of the Jordan." To meet the requirements that everyone - who needed it - could get to a city of refuge, three were needed on each side of the river, regardless of the relative population density, because of the distances involved.

The עָרֵי מִקְלָט, cities of refuge, were a device that *HaShem* ordained to provide a safe haven for those who had accidentally killed another person. The etymology of the word is both straightforward and obscure: a מ prefix is commonly added to verb roots to designate the place where an action takes place. An example of this is the root זָבַח - to slaughter or sacrifice - which produces the noun מִזְבֵּחַ - an altar - the place of sacrifice. The root קָלַט is used sufficiently infrequently in the Hebrew Bible that Davidson offers only an Arabic "to contract" or an Aramaic "to receive" meaning. Jastrow lists "to cut" or "to kill" for rabbinic Hebrew; Brown-Driver-Briggs gives "to be stunted". The noun, though, has an undisputed meaning of "refuge" or "reception", indicating not only that someone could flee there to find refuge, but that they would be received or accepted there by the people of the cities.

The prophets speak on a number of occasions about God being a refuge. "For You have been a refuge for the poor, a refuge for the needy in distress, shelter from the storm, shade from the heat - for the blast from the ruthless was like a storm that could destroy a wall" (Isaiah 25:4, CJB), "Adonai, my strength, my fortress, my refuge in time of trouble" (Jeremiah 16:19, CJB), "And the LORD roars from Zion and utters His voice from Jerusalem, and the heavens and the earth tremble. But the LORD is a refuge for His people and a stronghold to the sons of Israel" (Joel 3:9, NASB). The Psalmist makes use of the same image in very similar words: "The LORD is my rock, my fortress, and my deliverer, my God, my rock in whom I take refuge, my shield, and the horn of my salvation, my stronghold" (Psalm 18:2, NRSV), while Solomon also bring wisdom: "Fear of the LORD is a stronghold, a refuge for a man's children" (Proverbs 14:26, JPS).

Yeshua welcomed all those who came to Him, seeking refuge or simply acceptance. The gospels do not record a single instance of Him turning away anyone who was truly seeking to know Him. Famously, He said, "Come to Me, all who are weary and heavy-laden, and I will give you rest. Take My yoke upon you, and learn from Me, for I am gentle and humble in heart; and you shall find rest for your souls. For My yoke is easy, and My load is light" (Matthew 11:28-30, NASB). Matthew also applies the prophecy: "A battered reed He will not break off, and a smoldering wick He will not put out" (Matthew 12:20, NASB, from Isaiah 42:3) to Yeshua. He continues to be our refuge and strength: "My sheep hear My voice, and I know them, and they follow Me; and I give eternal life to them, and they shall never perish; and no one shall snatch them out of My hand. My Father, who has given them to Me, is greater than all; and no one is able to snatch them out of the Father's hand" (John 10:27-29, NASB). He is our security and our future, our vision and our purpose: "All that the Father gives Me shall come to Me, and the one who comes to Me I will certainly not cast out. For I have come down from heaven, not to do My own will, but the will of Him who sent Me. And this is the will of Him who sent Me, that of all that He has given Me I lose nothing, but raise it up on the last day" (John 6:37-39, NASB).

Further Study: Isaiah 42:1-3; Psalm 31:1-6

Application: Are you battered by the storms of this world and know that you need a refuge, a strong place to hide and find peace with God? Then look no further: Yeshua is the one for You. He is our city of refuge and He guarantees to receive us.

B'Midbar - Numbers

Shavuot - Weeks

Traditional "Festival Readings" are allocated for the two days of *Shavuot*. Our readings are taken from both the traditional readings and other ancient sources.

רִאשׁוֹן   Drash One   D'varim/Deuteronomy 16:11

שֵׁנִי   Drash Two   Shemot/Exodus 19:1

Shavuot - Weeks -1

D'varim / Deuteronomy 16:11

D'varim/Deuteronomy 16:11 you, your son, your daughter, your servant, your maid-servant, the Levite ... the alien, the orphan and the widow ...

אַתָּה וּבִנְךָ וּבִתֶּךָ וְעַבְדְּךָ וַאֲמָתֶךָ וְהַלֵּוִי
v'haleyvi va'amatecha v'avd'cha oovitecha oovincha atah

... וְהַיָּתוֹם וְהָאַלְמָנָה
v'ha'almanah v'hayatom ...

    This is the list of people who are to rejoice before the Lord at the feast of *Shavuot* each year at the end of the first harvest season, at the end of the period known as the Counting of the *Omer*, fifty days from *Pesach*. The full text reads: "And you shall rejoice before the Lord your God - you, your son, your daughter, your slave/servant, your maid-servant, the Levite who is in your gates, the alien, the orphan and the widow who is in your midst, in the place where Adonai your God will choose to dwell His name there". **Rashi**, incorporating the Sages before him, comments: "My four corresponding to your four ... if you will make mine happy, I will make yours happy" (**Tanchuma** 18). The two groups of four - those in a household and those outside a normal household - demonstrates how tightly integrated the immediate and the extended families are intended to work within God's community.

    The Levites, who lived among the other tribes, but without a land inheritance, were dependent on God to provide for them by way of the tithes of the people and their share in the offerings at the temple. The aliens, widows and orphans, without even that statutory provision that the Levites were supposed to enjoy, were nevertheless specifically included in the social economy of the nation Israel. Here, in this verse, God makes three interesting points: firstly that those outside the normal household and family structures are to be explicitly included in the rejoicing at this feast-time; secondly that the rejoicing will be incomplete or invalid if the disadvantaged are not included and embraced within the celebration; and thirdly, by implication, that the measure of the rejoicing - whether everyone is actually able to enjoy it - is directly related to the degree that everyone is included.

When he was describing how he was commissioned by the apostles in Jerusalem to take the gospel to the Gentiles, Rav Sha'ul wrote that, "they only asked us to remember the poor - the very thing I also was eager to do" (Galatians 2:10, NASB). James adds: "the religious observance that God the Father considers pure and faultless is this: to care for orphans and widows in their distress" (James 1:27, CJB). Four categories are covered by Zechariah: "Don't oppress widows, orphans, foreigners or poor people" (Zechariah 7:10, CJB) while Isaiah brings God's word to define the way that the people should behave to the people of his time: "Learn to do good! Seek justice, relieve the oppressed, defend orphans, plead for the widow" (Isaiah 1:17, CJB). God's heart for His people is that everyone from the rich down to the poor, from the able-bodied to the disabled, from families to orphans, widows, singles and the childless, is that they should all be included in His family and have reason to rejoice before Him.

Further Study: Psalm 146:7-9; Luke 14:12-14

Application: Whether you feel yourself to be on the outside, longing for someone to invite you in, or whether you have been blessed with substance to share with others in God's economy, know that God's family is meant to be inclusive and that you are called to reach out to and with those around you and share and rejoice together.

B'Midbar - Numbers

Shavuot - Weeks - 2

Shemot / Exodus 19:1

Shemot/Exodus 19:1 In the third month ... in this day, they entered the Sinai wilderness

בַּחֹדֶשׁ הַשְּׁלִישִׁי ... בַּיּוֹם הַזֶּה בָּאוּ מִדְבַּר
bakhodesh hashlishiy ... bayom hazeh ba'u midbar

סִינָי:
Siynay

    In the Pesikta de Rab Kahana, Rabbi Abu begins his *Shavuot* talk by quoting a verse from Proverbs: "Have I not, with counsel and knowledge, written for you noble things" (Proverbs 22:20). The word translated "noble things" is one of those that are written one way but traditionally read in a different way. In this case the word is written שלשום, but pronounced שָׁלִישִׁים and most translators follow the reading rather than the writing. Not so Rabbi Abu, who suggests that the written word means "as though it were only the day before yesterday." According to Rabbi Eleazer, the *Torah* should not look like an anticipated decree, but like a decree freshly issued which all rush to read. Rabbi - often taken to be Rabbi Judah, the compiler of the Mishnah - added, "freshly issued, not more than two or three days ago for שלשם means 'the day before yesterday'". Ben Azzai will have none of this; "Not even as old as a decree issued two or three days ago, but as a decree issued this very day - this is the way to regard the *Torah*." This is why our text - describing the arrival of the Children of Israel in the Sinai wilderness - explicitly says "on this day" rather than "on that day", because the text is emphasising the "now" nature of the narrative and the way it is to be interpreted. Just as in the *Pesach Hagaddah* the text says that each generation is to consider that they were freed from Egypt, so the text is hinting that we should all think, fifty days later, that we arrived at Mount Sinai in order to hear the words of the *Torah* spoken to us personally.

    As Moshe is rehearsing the *Torah* forty years later with the generation who are about to enter the Land, he says to them, "This day the Lord your

God commands you to do these statutes and ordinances. You shall therefore be careful to do them with all your soul" (D'varim 26:16, NASB). Even though some of the people would have been able to remember that day, when they were children, Moshe doesn't refer to it as a past event that has already happened, but as a present "now" event; *HaShem* is still commanding His people to obey His *Torah*. For the people hearing Moshe speak, *HaShem* is placing a call on their hearts "today"; today they are to obey Him. As he starts his summing up, three chapters later, Moshe tells the people, "You stand today, all of you, before the Lord your God: your chiefs, your tribes, your elders and your officers, all the men of Israel, your little ones, your wives, and the alien who is in your camps, from the one who chops your wood down to the one who draws your water, that you may enter into covenant with the Lord your God, and into His oath which the Lord your God is making with you today" (29:10-12, NASB).

Wait a minute! Didn't Moshe inaugurate the covenant at Sinai as an everlasting covenant, a permanent agreement and obligation, binding upon all generations of Jews for all time? Didn't our people speak with one voice and say, "All the words which the Lord has spoken we will do!" (Shemot 24:3, NASB), before Moshe took blood and sprinkled it on the people saying, "Behold the blood of the covenant, which the Lord has made with you in accordance with all these words" (v. 8, NASB). So what are the people doing now, forty years afterwards? As Moshe teaches and explains the covenant again in the next generation, they too have to enter into it for themselves, they too have to hear and acknowledge it by responding, "we shall hear and do" what *HaShem* is commanding us.

In his next breath Moshe goes on, "Now not only with you alone am I making this covenant and this oath, but with those who stand here with us in the presence of the Lord our God and with those who are not here with us today" (D'varim 29:14-15, NASB). This is a multi-generational covenant that the people are to review, re-enter and keep in every generation. Each person is to consider that they personally stood at Sinai and heard God speaking, that they not only said but continue to say, "we will do everything God says". By this we keep the covenant alive and fresh; by this we prevent the *Torah* becoming stale; by this God's word stays "living and active, sharper than any two-edged sword" (Hebrews 4:12, NASB).

Fifteen hundred years after the giving of the *Torah* at Mount Sinai, the disciples of Yeshua crowded each day into the upper room in Jerusalem to meet for prayer. Yeshua had been with them for forty days since his resurrection (Acts 1:3) and had left them to wait out the time until the feast of *Shavuot*, counting the last seven days of the *Omer* until the day of the feast itself came. Suddenly, "there came from heaven a noise like a violent, rushing wind, and it filled the whole house where they were sitting" (Acts 2:2, NASB). With tongues of fire on their heads and speaking in other tongues, they were filled with the Spirit of God, as were the prophets of old. The written *Torah* that they had been fulfilling for the last fifty days as they counted the days from Passover to *Shavuot*, first with Yeshua and then by themselves during the last week, suddenly became the living *Torah* as the Holy Spirit flowed through them. Suddenly their world was turned upside down as they were filled with assurance, power, understanding and praise for God that flowed through them so quickly that they couldn't stop it. No wonder the people in the streets around thought at first they were drunk!

Today, another two thousand years on, for many the story has become nothing more than that: a story. Many believers fail to connect with the now-ness of God because they see Him in history, as past events that were exciting if you were there, but aren't really relevant today to the pressures and sophistications of a modern world. Modern and post-modern people are focussed upon themselves, unable or unwilling to break out of the norms of society and stand up for the truths of the Bible and the reality of relationship with God, infused and empowered by the Holy Spirit. Now is the time; today is the day and God is waiting for each one of us to open ourselves up to Him, to take the risk of making a covenant afresh for ourselves with the living God. This is the call on our lives today: live dangerously, stand up to be counted, dare to be different - proclaim the reality of God in a hurting and broken world!

Further Study: Luke 11:27-28; Joshua 1:1-9

Application: Do you long for more in your relationship with God? This Pentecost, reach out to Him and claim the promise that "is for you and your children, and to all who are far off, as many as the Lord our God shall call to Himself" (Acts 2:39, NASB).

Biographies

Ba'al HaTurim - Rabbi Yaakov ben Asher, 1269-1343, born in Cologne, Germany; lived for 40 years in and around Toledo, Spain; died *en route* to Israel; his commentary to the Chumash is based upon an abridgement of the Ramban, including Rashi and Ibn Ezra; it includes many references to *gematria* and textual novelties

HaDarshan - Rabbi Moshe HaDarshan, an 11th century *Rosh Yeshiva* in Narbonne, Provence

Hirsch - Rabbi Samson Raphael Hirsch, 1808-1888, German rabbi of Frankfurt am Main, author and educator; staunch opponent of the Reform movement in Germany and one of the fathers of Orthodox Judaism

Ibn Ezra - Abraham Ibn Ezra, 1089-1167, born in Tudela, Spain; died in the South of France after wandering all around the shores of the Mediterranean and England; a philosopher, astronomer, doctor, poet and linguist; wrote a Hebrew grammar and a commentary on the Bible

Maharal - Judah Loew ben Bezalel, 1520-1609, known as the Maharal of Prague; a writer on Jewish philosophy mysticism and a super-commentary on Rashi

Nechama Leibowitz - 1905-1997, born in Riga, graduate of the University of Berlin, made *aliyah* in 1931; professor at Tel Aviv University; taught *Torah* for over 50 years

Rabbi Akiva - Akiva ben Joseph, c.50-c.135; one of the third generation of the Mishnaic Sages, who were active between 70 and 135; although starting life as an ignorant shepherd, he became perhaps the most central authority quoted in the *Mishnah*; known by some as the "father of the Rabbinic Judaism"

Rabbi Tarfon - one of the third generation of the Mishnaic Sages; actually served in the 2nd Temple and pronounced the Aaronic Benediction there; an adherent of the school of Shammai yet with a reputation for leniency

Rambam - Rabbi Moshe ben Maimon or Maimonedes, 1135-1204, Talmudist, philosopher, astronomer and physician; author of *Mishneh Torah*, Guide for the Perplexed and other works; a convinced rationalist

Ramban - Rabbi Moshe ben Nachman of Gerona or Nachmanides, 1194-1270, Spanish rabbi, author and physician; defended Judaism in the Christian debates in Barcelona before making *aliyah* to *Eretz Yisrael*

The Rashba - Rabbi Shlomo ben Aderet, 1235-1310CE, rabbi, halakhist and Talmudist; born and lived all his life in Barcelona and became a successful banker and leader of Spanish Jewry; his teachers include the Ramban; wrote a commentary on the *Torah* and over 3000 responsa; defended the Rambam's work but was opposed to rationalist philosophy; taught against false messianism

Rashi - Rabbi Shlomo Yitzchaki, 1040-1105, French rabbi who wrote commentaries on the *Torah*, the Prophets and the *Talmud*, lived in Troyes where he founded a *yeshiva* in 1067; perhaps the best-known of all Jewish commentators; focuses on the plain meaning (*p'shat*) of the text, although sometimes quite cryptic in his brevity

Resh Lakish - Simeon ben Lakish, a third century teacher who lived in Sephoris, long-time study partner of Rabbi Yochanan

Sa'adia Gaon - Sa'adis ben Yosef of Faym, 882/892 Egypt - 942 Bagdad; a prominent rabbi, Jewish philosopher, and exegete of the Geonic period

Sforno - Rabbi Ovadiah Sforno, 1470-1550, Italian rabbi, philosopher and physician; born in Cesena, he went to Rome to study medicine; left in 1525 and after some years of travel, settled in Bologna where he founded a *yeshiva* which he conducted until his death

Bibliography

Books by Author

Abraham Even-Shoshan, *A New Concordance of the Bible*, Kiryat Sefer Publishing House, Jerusalem 1988 (Hebrew only)

Benjamin Davidson, *The Analytical Hebrew and Chaldee Lexicon*, Samuel Bagster & Sons Ltd, London 1850

Brown, Driver and Briggs, *Hebrew and English Lexicon*, HoughtonMiflin and Company, Boston 1906

Dallas Willard, *The Divine Conspiracy*, HarperOne, 1998

David Bivin, *New Light on The Difficult Words of Jesus*, En-Gedi Resource Center, 2005

Israel Drazin & Stanley M Wagner, *Onkelos on the Torah - Numbers*, Gefen Publishing House, Jerusalem 2009

Jacob Milgrom, *The JPS Torah Commentary - B'midbar*, Jewish Publication Society, Philadelphia 1992

Marcus Jastrow, *Dictionary of the Targumim, Talmud Bavli and Yerushalmi and Midrashic Literature*, Hendrickson Publishers Inc, 2004

Richard Elliott Friedman, *Commentary on the Torah*, Harper Collins, San Francisco 2003

Books by Title

Authorised Daily Prayer Book, New translation and Commentary by Chief Rabbi Dr. Lord Jonathan Sacks, Harper Collins, London 2006

B'midbar Rabbah - one of the components of the *Midrash Rabbah* collection (the Great Midrash), probably compiled in the eleventh or twelfth centuries CE. Drawing on *Midrash Tanchuma* and work by Rabbi Moshe HaDarshan, it cites many comments and opinions of the early Sages

B'resheet Rabbah - one of the components of the *Midrash Rabbah*

collection (the Great Midrash), probably compiled around 400-450 CE in *Eretz Yisrael* from the oral teachings of many of the early sages - some named, some anonymous - in the previous 400 years

BHS - Biblia Hebraica Stuttgartensia, the standard eclectic/scholarly text of the Hebrew Scriptures, German Bible Society 1997

Devek Tov - a super-commentary to Rashi's *Torah* commentary, written by Simeon b. Isaac ha-Levi in 1588

Midrash Rabbah - a collection of *aggadic* commentaries upon the *Torah* and some other books of the Bible most used in worship; different volumes have been collated in written form between the 4th and 13th centuries CE; they contain both very early oral material from the sages of the 1st and 2nd centuries and glosses and inserts down to the 1200s

Midrash Tanchuma - a collection of *midrashim* on the *Torah* collected and published in the ninth century

Mishnah - the collection of Jewish law and customs codified (collected and written down) under the auspices of Rabbi Judah the Prince around the year 200 CE

Mizrachi - a super-commentary on Rashi written by Elijah Mizrachi, 1455-1525, born in Constantinople, in 1495 became Grand Rabbi of the Ottoman empire

Pesikta de Rab Kahana - a collection of *midrash* and sermons for the special sabbaths and the festivals throughout the year; the oldest material comes from the 1st and 2nd centuries but the collection was probably redacted in the late 4th or early 5th century

Pirkei Avot - literally "Chapters of the Fathers", although usually "Ethics of the Fathers"; one of the tractates of the *Mishnah* that includes many pithy proverb-like sayings attributed to the sages who contributed to the *Mishnah*

Septuagint - Also known simply as LXX, the Septuagint is a translation of the whole of the Hebrew Scriptures into Greek that was probably done during the 1st century BCE by members of the Jewish community in Alexandria to have the Scriptures in their "first" tongue; the quality is mixed - some parts, such as the *Torah*, were in frequent use and are quite well rendered, other parts were less used and the translation is rather patchy and shows signs of haste; it was widely deprecated by the early rabbis who generated the story of its being translated under threat of death by 70 Jewish scholars on the orders of Ptolemy

Sifre - the earliest rabbinic commentary to the books of B'Midbar and D'varim; probably composed of two parts, one from the Schools of Rabbi Simeon and Rabbi Ishmael, the other from the School of Rabbi Akiva; the earliest material dates from 100-150 CE, but there are later additions until Talmudic times

Sifsei Chachamim - a super-commentary to Rashi's commentary on the Pentateuch; written by Shabbetai ben Joseph Bass, 1641-1718, an educated man and printer of Jewish books in Breslau

Sim Shalom - named after the last stanza of the *Amidah*, the official prayer-book of Conservative Judaism: The Rabbinical Assembly, *Sim Shalom*, New York City 2001

Talmud - literally, instruction or learning; the distilled writings of the early sages, a composite of the *Mishnah* and the *Gemarah*, an extensive commentary to the *Mishnah*; two talmuds exist: the Jerusalem Talmud, from around 400-450, compiled in the Land of Israel; and the Babylonian Talmud, from around 550-600, compiled in the Jewish communities in Babylon

Tanakh - the Hebrew Scriptures: *Torah* (Instructions/Law), *Nevi'im* (Prophets) and *Ketuvim* (Writings)

Glossary

Adonai - literally, "My Lord" or "My Master"; although appearing in the Hebrew text as a word in its own right, it is widely used as a elusive synonym to avoid pronouncing the tetragrammaton - יהוה - the ineffable or covenant name of God; where the latter appears in a text, and is being read in a worship context, it will be pronounced as *Adonai*

Aleinu - the paryaer recited at the end of the three daily prayer services; traditionally created and proclaimed by Joshua; praises God for allowing the Jewish people to serve Him and affirms the End Times expectations of Judaism (and Christianity)

aliyah (pl. *aliyot*) - literally "going up"; used as the name for one (or more) of the seven sections in which the *Torah* portion is read on *Shabbat*; so named because (1) the reader ascends physically to the *bimah* or platform in the synagogue to read and (2) the reader ascends spiritually by reading from the *Torah*

Amidah - The Standing Prayer, see *Shemoneh Esrei*

anthropomorphism - ascribing human qualities - emotions, attributes or physical characteristics - to God or an inanimate object

Aramaic - a member of the Northwest family of Semitic languages, heavily cognate with Hebrew. Aramaic script - also known as Assyrian Square Script - replaced the earlier paeo-Hebrew script which was more like Phoenician in appearance. The majority of the *Talmud* is written in Aramaic as are parts of Daniel and Ezra

b'rakhah - a blessing

Chazal - an acronym: "Ch" stands for "Chachameinu", Our Sages, and the "z" and "l" correspond to the expression "Zichronam Livrocho", "of blessed memory"; this is a catch-all that often refers to the authoritative opinion in the Talmud, sometimes just the collected wisdom of the Sages in years past

cohen (pl. *cohanim*) - priest, so *cohen gadol* or *Cohen HaGadol*, the High Priest

Diaspora - from a Greek word meaning to scatter or disperse, this is the name given to the Jewish people scattered in exile throughout the world, as opposed to the part of the Jewish people that live in *Eretz Yisrael*

Eretz Yisrael - the Land of Israel

Gei Hinnom - anglicised as 'Gehenna', literally the Hinnom valley, just outside Jerusalem; used as a synoym for Hell

gematria - a system of assigning a numerical value to a Hebrew word or phrase (using the numerical values of the letter) in order to connect it to other words and phrases having the same numerical value; produces some interesting results but can be abused to generate spurious connections

ger (pl. gerim) - foreign resident, sojourner, alien; in Orthodox Judaism today, this word can also be read as a convert to Judaism

Goyim - the nations

Haftarah - literally, "leave taking"; the reading from the Prophets or Writings that follows the reading from the *Torah*; thematically linked to the *Torah* reading, some of these have been set since the Babylonian exile

halacha - literally "the walking"; the detailed case law of implementing *Torah*

Hannuukah - the eight-day feast, starting on the twenty-fifth of *Kislev*, commemorating the victory of the Maccabees over the Greeks in *Eretz Yisrael* in the second century BCE; mentioned in John 10:22 as the Feast of Dedication

hapax legomenon - Greek phrase meaning "something said once"; a word that has only one instance of use within a body of literature; in the Bible, a word that either is only used once, in any form, or - less strictly - a particular form that is only used once

HaShem - literally, "The Name"; widely used as a elusive synonym to avoid pronouncing the tetragrammaton - יהוה - the ineffable or covenant name of God; where this appears in a text, and is not being read in a worship context, it will be pronounced as *HaShem*

Hif'il and *Hof'al* - the causitive voices (active and passive, respectively) of a

Hebrew verb

Hitpa'el - the reflexive or iterative voice of a Hebrew verb

kabbalah - literally, "receiving", teaching and school of thought concerned with the mystical aspect of Judaism. Emerged 11th - 13th century CE in Spain, recast in *Eretz Yisrael* in the 16th century

kosher - literally, "approved"; something, typically food, that meets the appropriate regulations; the term *glatt kosher* (the Yiddish word *glatt* means 'smooth') is informally used to denote food prepared to the strictest kosher regulations

lulav & etrog - the four species, waved during the Feast of *Sukkot* to fulfill Vayikra 23:40; the lulav is a frond of date palm and includes the myrtle and the willow, and the etrog is a citron

masorete - the Masoretes were groups of scribes and scholars in Tiberias and Jerusalem - *masorete* meaning guardian or keeper of tradition - in the 8th - 9th centuries CE; they preserved the traditional pronunciation, chanting and breathing of the Hebrew Bible text, lest it should be lost and future generations unable to read and interpret the consonantal text

Masoretic Text - the standard Jewish text of the Hebrew Bible, as annotated with vowels and trope marks by the *Masoretes* in the 9th century CE; devised by Aharon ben Moshe ben Asher in Tiberias, these pointed texts are preserved in the Aleppo Codex (930 CE) and the Leningrad Codex (1008 CE)

matzah (pl. *matzot*) - unleaved bread; flat bread made without yeast

metzora - a person who has been examined by a *cohen* and declared impure on the basis of the symptoms of *tzara'at*.

mezuzah (pl. *mezuzot)* - literally, doorpost; a container afixed to the right-hand side of a door-frame, holding a small parchment with some of the words of the *Sh'ma*.

Midrash (pl. *midrashim*) - literally, study or investigation; the technique of *Midrash* is to interpret or study texts based on textual issues, links to other verses and narratives; as a class it includes both *halachic* (law-based) and *aggadic* (story or narrative) material which often fills in many gaps in the biblical material *minyan* - the 'quorum' of ten men deemed necessary to represent the community for reciting many of the prayers in the daily prayer services

Mishkan - literally, "place of dwelling/presence"; the Tabernacle

mitzvah (pl. *mitzvot*) - literally, command or commandments

Niphal - the passive voice of a Hebrew verb

Olam Haba - the world to come

Olam Hazeh - the present world

Omer - literally, "sheaf"; a dry volume measure for grain; used for counting the fifty days of the barley harvest between *Pesach* and *Shavuot*

parasha (pl. *parashiyot*) - one of the traditional names for the divisions into weekly portions of the Hebrew Bible; the *Torah* contains 54 portions, each with its own name taken from one of the first few words in the text

Pesach - Passover

Pesach Hagaddah - the order of words and actions that take place at a Passover seder; compiled originally between 170 and 280 CE, tradition suggests by Rabbi Judah himself; the oldest complete manuscript dates to the 10th century

Pi'el and *Pu'al* - the emphatic or stressed voices (active and passive, respectively) of a Hebrew verb

P'rushim - Pharisees

Qal - literally, "light"; the unmodified or unenhanced version of a Hebrew verb; the simplest meaning of a Hebrew verb root

Qohelet - the Hebrew name for the book of Ecclesiastes

Rosh Chodesh - literally, "head of the month"; the day of the New Moon feast, to be marked by the blowing of silver trumpets; declared by the *Sanhedrin* in Jerusalem after having received reliable testimony from two witnesses that the new moon has been sighted

Rosh HaShana - literally, "head of the year"; the first day of Tishrei, the seventh month in the Jewish year, also known as *Yom Teruah*, the Day of Blowing; used as the civil New Year

Rosh Yeshiva - the principle or headmaster of a *Yeshiva*, rabbinical school

Ruach HaKodesh - literally, "Spirit or Breath, the Holy"; most common Hebrew name for the Holy Spirit

Sanhedrin - the most senior court in biblical Israel, with seventy one members; recently re-founded in the modern state of Israel

seder - literally, "order"; a formal liturgical remembrance and meal; most familiarly the Passover Seder, 3 hours of liturgy and ritual actions to remember the Exodus from Egypt; also *Shavuot* Seder and Tu B'Shevat Seder

Sh'ma - the first word of D'varim 6:4; an imperative verb: Hear!; the name of the primary Jewish statement of faith: Hear O Israel, the Lord, our God, the Lord is One

Shabbat - the 24 hours from sunset Friday to sunset Saturday, the seventh day of the week; literally, "the ceasing" because as Jews we cease any kind of work during those hours

Shabbat Shekalim - the day each year when the half-shekel tax for the upkeep of the Temple was collected; now set as the *shabbat* before the first of Adar (Adar II in a leap year); the *Torah* portion Shemot 30:11-16 is read

Shabbat Shuva - the *shabbat* that falls between *Yom Teruah (Rosh HaShana)* and *Yom Kippur* each year; so called from the *Haftarah* portion which is read: Hosea 14:2-10, starting with the imperative verb *Shuva*, Return!

shabbaton - loosely translated 'sabbatical' and may be used for a year, a month or an arbitrary time period; also used for 'sabbath' as a class rather than one particular *shabbat*

Shacharit - literally "dawn"; the name of the early morning prayer service

Shavuot - literally "weeks"; the name of the bibical Feast of Weeks at the end of the fifty days of the counting the *Omer* (sheaf) from *Pesach*

(Passover)

Shemoneh Esrei - literally, "The Eighteen" because it originally contained eighteen stanzas or blessings; the central prayer of the three daily prayer services. Also known as the *Amidah* - "standing" or simply "the prayer", the rabbis determined that this prayer was the act of service that replaced the sacrifices in worship after the destruction of the Second Temple

shofar - ram's horn trumpet

Siddur - the standard Jewish prayer book or order of daily prayers; extant in many oral and traditional forms before 800 CE, first codified by Sa'adia Gaon around 850 CE, first printed 1486 CE in Italy; contains the basic fixed contents of the prayer services

Sh'ma - the first word of D'varim 6:4; an imperative verb: Hear!; the name of the primary Jewish statement of faith: Hear O Israel, the Lord, our God, the Lord is One.

sukkah (pl. *sukkot*) - booth or shelter

Sukkot - the Feast of Tabernacles

talmid (pl. *talmidim*) - student or disciple

Tanna - Hebrew, literally, "repeater or teacher"; one of the rabbinic sages whose views are recorded in the *Mishnah*; active from around 70 - 200 CE

Targum - literally, translation or interpretation; two principle *targums* are known: *Targum Onkelos*, a translation with some paraphrase of the *Torah* into Aramaic; *Targum Jonathan*, a translation with rather more paraphrase of the Prophets into Babylonian Aramaic. *Targum Neofiti* is a third *targum* in Palestinian Aramaic. They were probably made between 200-400 and were used in the reading and study of the Hebrew scriptures: one line or verse in Hebrew, followed by the same line or verse from the *Targum*. Important early witnesses to the text and translation into a closely connected cognate language

tetragrammaton - the four letter covenant name of God: יהוה yod-hay-vav-hay; never pronounced as written within the Jewish tradition and never vowelised with a correct set of vowels to prevent pronunciation

Torah - the first in the three parts of the Hebrew Bible (with Prophets and Writings); from the root יָרָה, to throw or teach; often translated 'law' but probably better 'instruction'; used at a minimum to describe the five books of Moshe, often expanded to include the whole of the Hebrew Bible, the *Talmud* and the Jewish writings, so that it can be used as a totally encompassing term

tzaddik - a righteous man

tzara'at - Hebrew word for skin disease; often translated - incorrectly, since it bears no relationship to the latter disease - as leprosy

tzitzit (pl. *tzitziyot*) - tassels; worn (as per B'Midbar 15:38-40) on the four corners of a garment

yeshiva (pl. *yeshivot*) - Jewish religious school/college where the syllabus is almost exclusively studying the *Torah* and the Jewish writings

Yishuv - literally, settlement; the Old Yishuv refers to Jews in *Eretz Yisrael* before approximately 1882, mainly living in estabished cities; the New/Young Yishuv refers to Jews who made *aliyah* btween 1882 and 1948 and built outside the old city walls, the *kibbutzim*

Yom HaBikkurim - Day of Early Firstfruits, the day during the Festival of *Matzot* when the first sheaf was cut and offered as a wave offering in the Temple

Yom Kippur - the Day of Atonement

B'Midbar - Numbers

Author Biography

Although professionally trained and qualified as a software engineer, Jonathan's calling to the Messianic Jewish ministry started in the mid-90s after a season of serving as a local preacher in the churches of North Devon. He was ordained "Messianic Rabbi" by Dr Daniel Juster and Tikkun Ministries, and has served as a Tikkun network congregational leader in England for some years. Now the founder and director of Messianic Education Trust - an educational charity and ministry that works to share the riches of the Jewish background of our faith in Messiah with the church, while teaching Yeshua as the Jewish messiah - he lives in the south-west of England with his wife, Belinda, and three of his four daughters. There he contributes to the local body of believers by being involved in the Exeter Street Pastors project.

You can follow the work of Messianic Education Trust and read the weekly commentaries as they are produced each week, on the MET website at:

http://www.messianictrust.org

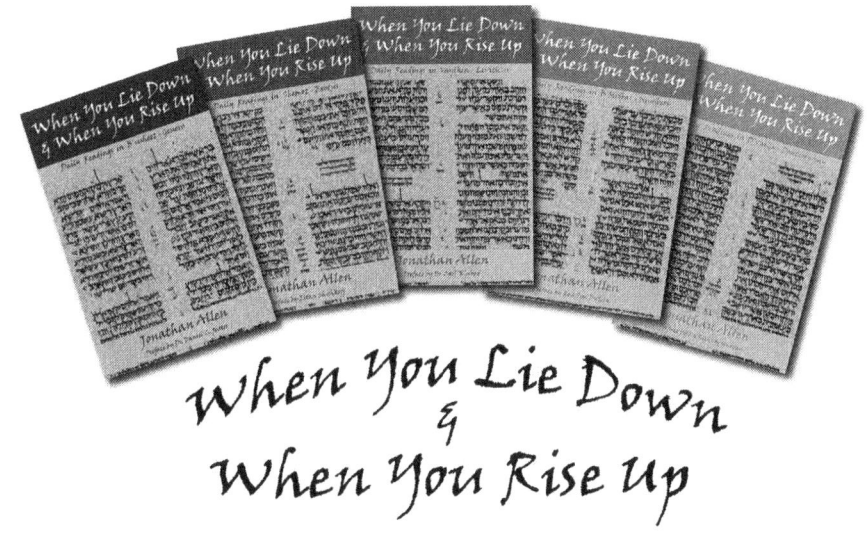

When You Lie Down & When You Rise Up

Daily Readings Following The Weekly Torah Portions

Rabbi Jonathan Allen

Daily Readings in B'resheet - Genesis - 1-901917-09-6

Daily Readings in Shemot - Exodus - 1-901917-10-X

Daily Readings in Vayikra - Leviticus - 1-901917-11-8

Daily Readings in B'Midbar - Numbers - 1-901917-12-6

Daily Readings in Devarim - Deuteronomy - 1-901917-13-4

www.elishevapublishing.co.uk